NOT ALWAYS IN THE MOOD

NOT ALWAYS IN THE MOOD

The New Science of Men, Sex, and Relationships

Sarah Hunter Murray

ROWMAN & LITTLEFIELD
Lanham • Boulder • New York • London

Published by Rowman & Littlefield
An imprint of The Rowman & Littlefield Publishing Group, Inc.
4501 Forbes Boulevard, Suite 200, Lanham, Maryland 20706
www.rowman.com

6 Tinworth Street, London SE11 4AL

British Library Cataloguing in Publication Information Available

Library of Congress Cataloging-in-Publication Data

Name: Murray, Sarah Hunter, 1984–, author.
Title: Not always in the mood : the new science of men, sex, and relationships / Sarah Hunter Murray.
Description: Lanham : Rowman & Littlefield, [2019] | Includes bibliographical references and index.
Identifiers: LCCN 2018029440 (print) | LCCN 2018030615 (ebook) | ISBN 9781538113943 (elec-
    tronic) | ISBN 9781538113936 (cloth : alk. paper)
Subjects: LCSH: Men—Sexual behavior. | Men—Psychology. | Sex (Psychology) | Man–woman
    relationships.
Classification: LCC HQ28 (ebook) | LCC HQ28 .M87 2019 (print) | DDC 306.70811—dc23
LC record available at https://lccn.loc.gov/2018029440

∞ ™ The paper used in this publication meets the minimum requirements of
American National Standard for Information Sciences Permanence of Paper for
Printed Library Materials, ANSI/NISO Z39.48-1992.

Printed in the United States of America

To authentic relationships
and deeper sexual intimacy

CONTENTS

AUTHOR'S NOTES

1. The language I use in this book is representative of the people who informed and shaped my work. I acknowledge that gender is not a binary construct and that there is diversity in sexual orientation, sexual expression, and relationship configuration. My language use is not intended to be exclusionary. Instead, its intention is to tackle the dominant gender narratives that generally constrain many if not most of us, in particular cisgendered heterosexual sexual/romantic relational dynamics. As a result, where appropriate I use binary gender language (man and woman); binary biological terms (male and female); and heterosexual relationship structure (husband and wife, boyfriend and girlfriend). The vast majority of the empirical research I draw upon stems from challenging traditional gender roles that are mostly (although not exclusively) applicable to cisgendered heterosexual men. While I think it's unlikely that the findings I share in this book are reflective *only* of heterosexual men's experiences, I cannot conclusively state that there may not be slightly (or in some cases, greatly) different ways that gender-queer men and/or men in same-sex relationships experience sexual desire.

2. Out of respect for the privacy of the clients and research participants who entrusted me with their experiences, all stories in this book are composite, fictional accounts based on the experience of many individuals. Similarities to any real person or people are coincidental and unintentional.

3. This book is not intended as a therapy manual, nor is it intended to replace the advice of physicians or other licensed health professionals. Individual readers are solely responsible for their own health-care decisions and should consult a licensed health professional in such matters. Neither the publisher nor I accept responsibility for any adverse effects individuals claim to experience, whether directly or indirectly, from the information contained in this book.

ACKNOWLEDGMENTS

I am grateful to all the men and women in my research and clinical practice who shared their stories and experiences with me. You allowed me into your inner world and, in turn, revolutionized the way I think about intimate and romantic relationships. I am a better therapist, researcher, friend, and wife because of it.

I have been inspired, mentored, and bolstered by so many extraordinary professionals, including but in no way limited to Robin Milhausen, Cynthia Graham, Lynda Ashbourne, Olga Sutherland, Leon Kuczynski, Carolyn Pukall, Carolyn Klassen, Kristen Mark, Carm De Santis, Jessica Wood, Tricia van Rhijn, Kate Kiernan, Jasmin Finch, and Laura Cameron. I also want to thank my editor at *Psychology Today*, Matt Huston, for providing me with my first platform to shift from academic writing to writing for a broader audience.

I'm convinced I won the agent lottery with Lilly Ghahremani. Her infectious enthusiasm, insights, and vision for what I wanted to say helped polish and shape my ideas in a way that never would have been possible without her. Thanks to my editor at Rowman & Littlefield, Suzanne Staszak-Silva, for believing in my ideas and allowing me to share that knowledge with others.

I would also like to thank my parents and my sister, Hayley, for encouraging me in all my passions and endeavors, listening to my agonies and stresses, and picking me back up when my anxieties and self-doubts tried to get in the way. And thank you to my sister-in-law, Colleen, for pointing me in the most basic of ways to how to go about the process of writing a book.

Last but most of all, I want to thank my husband, Liam, for believing in me and encouraging me to write this book while we were on the dock that summer. You made me believe it was possible when I didn't know it myself.

INTRODUCTION

As a sex researcher beginning my career, it seemed only natural that I would study women. After all, *I am a woman.* I've talked with other women about intimacy, sex, and relationships my whole life. I know from years of experience, conversations, and confessions over a glass (or two) of wine that women's desire is complex, elusive, and completely worthy of study.

Women can feel horny one minute and then, in a millisecond, lose all interest. Women's sexual desire can feel hidden or nonexistent for weeks, only to show up suddenly during a sexy or romantic scene in a movie. Women's sexual desire is impacted by how connected we feel toward our partner[1] ("Have we spent time quality time together recently? Or is he sitting on a different couch, zoning out on his phone again?") and navigating confusing, dichotomous social messages[2] ("Don't be a prude" but also "Don't be a slut!"). Not to mention the role of medications, physical illnesses, sexual trauma, and the sexualization of women in the media.[3] Any one of these avenues could (and do) lead to a plethora of important research questions about women's sexuality.

But as I continued my research, I started to realize something: the complexities of women's sexual desire weren't being talked about, or studied, in isolation. Rather, women's sexual desire was often being *compared* and *contrasted* to men's sexual desire.

Researchers (including myself at one point, I must admit) felt justified in thinking that *women's* desire (implying, either implicitly or explicitly, that it was *unlike* men's desire) must be studied because it's complex and multifaceted. But no matter how the comparison was made, the assumption was always the same: *Women's desire is complex, while men's desire is straightforward. High. Constant. And simple.*

I saw it in therapy with my clients, too. Couples would start by making sweeping statements about how, obviously, *he* (like "all men") wanted frequent sex and *she* (like "all women") didn't have much sexual interest. We didn't need to focus on *him* because there was nothing to investigate. He was there for support. *She's* got the problem. Analyze her and figure out what's going on. And the women weren't disagreeing . . .

It goes without saying that these types of messages, where men are portrayed as "sex-crazed," simple creatures while women are seen as particular and finicky in their desire, are reiterated in TV shows, movies, and even conversations with friends or acquaintances on a fairly regular basis.

THE CONVERSATION THAT CHANGED EVERYTHING

Then one day I had a conversation that completely changed the way I think about men and sex. That day, like most days, my colleague and I were talking about sex and relationships when she said something casually, almost in passing:

> "My husband and I were talking with friends last night, and he said he was always in the mood for sex. But last weekend I suggested we have sex, and he said he was too tired. . . . What's that about?"

I think we said something like "Oh, that's men for you . . ." before our conversation turned to more pressing matters like our anxieties about publication deadlines and whether 10:00 a.m. was too early to go to the cafeteria for curly fries.

But the truth is, my thoughts lingered on that comment for a long time. In fact, I've never really stopped thinking about it . . .

If I were to take a guess, I would say that most women reading this have heard at least some guy (or perhaps even *several* guys) make a similar statement at some point in their lives—something along the lines of "*I'm* always in the mood for sex!" or "Anytime you want it, I'm ready!" And that most men reading this have probably uttered similar words at some point in their lives.

But didn't I know from my own relationships, and my friendships with men, that there were *of course* going to be times when men didn't feel desire or didn't want to have sex? That wasn't so far-fetched, was it? I mean, men are humans, not robots—right?

So why did those comments come up all the time? That men want sex "any time, any place, anywhere"? Did men really believe that when they said it? Was it simply bravado? For show? Or was there truth to it?

And what good came from men demonstrating this high, unwavering desire all the time anyway? From my experience researching women's sexual desire and working with women in therapy, the belief that their male partner wanted sex all the time was half the reason some women felt they had sexual problems in the first place! (Not to mention the reason a smaller, but perhaps more distressed, number of men came to therapy thinking they were "broken" from having desire that deviated from this stereotype.) I wondered . . .

- Was there a disconnect between what men *say* they want and what men *really* want?
- Was there a disconnect between what women *think* men want and what men *really* want?
- Was it possible that all these (potentially false) ideas about men and sex were getting in the way of heterosexual couples' sexual and intimate relationships?

My mind was spinning, and I knew I needed some answers.

THE (NOT SO) LONG AND WINDING ROAD

Being a sex researcher I dug in to find answers the best way I knew how. I committed to getting my hands on every single study about men's sexual desire I could find. And it didn't take me long to see that we certainly do make a lot of assumptions about men and sex.

In fact, the first thing I noticed was there was hardly any research about men's sexual desire to read! I'll be honest with you: as a nearly burnt-out graduate student my first reaction was "Perfect—less work for me!" But it didn't take long for my second reaction to kick in. Which was "Wait a second—why is there so little research for me to read?"

I came to realize that as researchers we have a blind spot about men and sex. Specifically, it seemed that the assumptions we hold about men's sexual desire are so engrained that we have barely taken the time to ask men about it. We assume that there is nothing complex going on, so why bother? It's *women's* desire that's complicated, remember?

So I decided right then that there was *something* going on with men's desire that we weren't talking about, something we weren't even bothering to ask. And if we were making those assumptions as researchers, we were making those assumptions *outside* of research. And then it just seemed natural that those assumptions, like any assumptions we hold, could be having a negative impact on us as men and women, and perhaps on our intimate relationships.

THE GLASS-SHATTERING REALIZATION

In *How I Met Your Mother*, there's one episode in which each character notices something new about the others—a "glass-shattering realization." Once this "thing" was noted about one of them, the rest of the group couldn't *stop* noticing it. For Robin it was that she said "literally" when she should have been saying "figuratively." For Lily it was that she crunched potato chips really loudly. Over the course of the episode those little idiosyncrasies no one had really noticed before became more and more obvious, until they couldn't be ignored and everyone cracked.

The same happened for me when the lid came off about our assumptions about men and sex.

I noticed more and more assumptions about men's desire being made everywhere I turned. I read research that would find small differences between men and women and then make sweeping statements that supported stereotypical norms about men's desire being high and women's desire being low (or complex, or elusive). I heard men in therapy *initially* describe themselves as having a high interest in sex, followed by numerous exceptions to the rule (or even admitting some of their desire was feigned rather than authentic). And I worked with more and more women who came to realize *their* sexual desire was perfectly healthy and normal, and misconceptions about what their *male partner's* desire "should" look like were responsible for them doubting themselves (or him, or even their relationship).

So I decided that I needed to talk to men directly and ask them about how they experienced sexual desire in their relationships. Over the course of my research and clinical practice, I've talked with business executives, truck drivers, schoolteachers, athletes, academic professionals, new dads, experienced dads. Men in their thirties, forties, fifties, and sixties. Men you might be uncomfortable passing in a dark alley and men who were gentle, awkward, and even a bit geeky. And over and over again I saw and heard the same thing: assumptions and expectations about men's sexual desire being constant, high, and unwavering are not working for men anymore, nor are they accurately portraying men's true sexual experiences. Just take a look at some statements I've heard from men:

> "I don't mind initiating sex with my girlfriend sometimes, but do I always have to be the one to do it? It would be nice to have her initiate sometimes; for her to show me that she wants me too."

> "If I ever turned down my wife when she wanted sex, she would be devastated. But why does she think it doesn't hurt when she says no to my sexual advances over and over again? Sometimes I feel like I shouldn't even try anymore."

> "My wife initiated sex last night but I had a long day at work and was just too tired and stressed out. I never thought I would turn down an opportunity to have sex. Is something wrong with me?"

> "My single friends say that I'm lucky because at least I'm having sex. But even though my wife and I have regular sex, I can tell she isn't that into it. Sometimes I'd rather not have sex at all than have sex with someone who is just waiting for it to be over."

THE MOMENTUM GREW

As I continued my quest to better understand men's sexuality, I realized I was far from the only one who wanted to know about men's sexual desire—their real, authentic experiences, not the narrow version we so often see portrayed in the media.

I could sense that when I spoke about this research, more than any other research I had done before, people's ears perked up. They wanted to know more. In fact, when I was sharing my findings for the first time, I was told the mood in the room changed when I began describing what men shared with me. The audience was leaning in. Taking notes! There was this curiosity: "I thought we knew all there was to know about men and sex. But do we really?"

I wondered if more folks might be interested in hearing this different perspective about men's sexual desire. So I pitched a blog idea to *Psychology Today* about challenging myths we hold about men and their desire. Almost immediately my now editor enthusiastically responded saying that their readers *needed* to know more about misconceptions concerning men and sex. So I began writing.

Once I started sharing my findings and observations, I learned that my blogs about men and sexual desire had five to ten times as many readers than any other topic I've written about (and I write about sex so I can assure you, it's all pretty fascinating!). I received e-mails, comments, and questions for interviews. Articles became syndicated on relationship and lifestyle blogs. Women e-mailed me with questions after reading one of my articles made them think differently about their male partner. Men shared links to the articles and said it was about time we had a conversation about there being more to men's desire (and men in general) than we were currently acknowledging.

It became clear that there was something going on here. There were things women wanted to know about their male partners, and things men were desperate for their female partners to be aware of when it came to sex.

I knew I was really on to something when in therapy I began playing around with giving more space for men to share their experiences of sexual desire. When men leaned on stereotypical masculine norms and then described exceptions to the rule, I gently questioned and challenged discrepancies. I asked men what they *really* got from sex, when they wanted it, and why. And more and more often, men talked about how sex was *so much more* than physical stimulation: they wanted to connect emotionally with their girlfriend or wife, to be seen and touched by her. They also shared that they didn't *always* feel in the mood.

Then I watched how the mood shifted. The women sitting in front of me were so often relieved and assured to know that sex was not just physical. That he *cared*. That she now understood his inner world a bit better. And that he took a risk to let her in. In fact, the women I talked to were (and are) often more open and receptive to their partner's sexual desire and more interested in sex themselves once they understand the complexities, nuances, and often relational side of their male partner's sexual desire. And that's because most women don't want a stereotypical hypermasculine man who just wants sex all the time, drinks beer, burps, and is void of emotion. Most women want a man they can relate to. A man they can communicate with. A man they understand and connect with.

IS THIS BOOK FOR ME?

The stereotypical masculine approach to sexual desire is working against heterosexual couples' intimate relationships, and it's getting in the way of good sex.

Women are either annoyed that it feels like their male partner *always* wants sex ("He wants sex now? Doesn't he know I've had a bad day?" Or "Can't he see I'm in the middle of watching this show?"), or they think their male partner *should* want sex all the time and are deeply concerned when he doesn't (like when he stops initiating sexual activity or turns down one—perhaps even several—of her sexual advances). Similarly, men are feeling increasingly frustrated by the pressure they face to play into narrow sexual stereotypes that depict them as simple and superficial. And more and more men want space to show, and be accepted for, the more human, emotional, and relational sides of their sexuality.

This book is for the woman who feels disconnected from her husband because it feels like he just wants sex. All. The. Freaking. Time. This book is for the woman who got all dressed up and whose boyfriend never made a move on her, leaving her baffled and disappointed. This book is for the woman who has been with her male partner for years and is feeling that things are just OK (or maybe even less than OK), and she wants to know him a little bit better.

This book is for the man who feels like his sexual virility isn't what it used to be and is doubting himself as a partner, man, and lover. This book is for the man who said no to sex for the first time in his life and is perplexed because in his single days he swore he would never, *ever* turn down a sexual opportunity. This book is for the man who feels like his sexual desire isn't quite what he thinks it "should" be and is starting to wonder, *am I normal?*

And this book is for the couple experiencing a sexual slump and feeling like they have exhausted every avenue related to figuring out what's "wrong" with her but maybe haven't fully considered whether the answers to better sex and closer connection might lie in better understanding and challenging outdated stereotypes about *his* desire.

This book addresses the underlying assumptions that result in these feelings and more. It shares a completely new perspective of men's sexual desire based on years of research and clinical conversations with men about sex and relationships. It demonstrates how we have been getting so much wrong about men and sex and how these far-reaching misconceptions are short-changing men, women, and our intimate relationships. By reading this book my hope is that you will . . .

Challenge assumptions about men and sex by shedding a much-needed light on men's inner emotional world—one that has been missing from our conversations about men and sex for far too long.

Have better sex. The underlying theme of this book is that men's sexual desire is motivated by their need to feel close and connected to their female partners. When *women* better understand men's sexual vulnerabilities, they often feel closer to their partner (and even feel more desire) because they see how sex is so much more to him than a physical act; it's an emotional bid for connection. When *men* are afforded the space to show the softer, more sensitive side of themselves, they have the opportunity to demonstrate their sexual desire in more authentic ways.

Improve your relationship. Our sex lives are incredibly intertwined with how happy and satisfied we feel in our romantic relationships.[4] This book offers a new and direct route for women and men to increase their intimate bond through challenging some of the biggest misconceptions and misperceptions about men and sex that cause rifts and disconnection in *and* out of the bedroom.

This book goes *so much further* than providing sexual tips and tricks that are so often stereotypically associated with men and sex. Rather, it's about men's inner psychological world. It's about how men *think* about sex and what men truly desire, in and out of the bedroom. This book challenges the stereotypical norms about men's sexual desire that limit *men's* sexual expressions and *women's* sexual enjoyment. And this book shows how reevaluating our perceptions about men and sex can lead to better sex and closer, more connected relationships.

Ready to get started?

THE ORIGIN OF MYTHS

Over the course of this book I'm going to debunk one myth after another about men's sexual desire. I will demonstrate how men's interest in sex is *anything* but simple and surface level, and how confronting our biggest misconceptions about men and sex can lead to more intimate romantic relationships and better, more satisfying sex. But, before we get to that, there is a big question that needs answering: *how did we come to hold these myths about men and sex in the first place?*

Well, there is a very good reason that so many of us believe the myth that men's sexual desire is strong, constant, simple, and unwavering (and, contrarily, why we tend to panic when men's desire comes across any other way). Because almost *everywhere* we turn we are inundated with messages that depict men as sex-crazed, insatiably horny creatures who always have sex on the brain, are easily turned on, and are ready for sex anytime, anywhere.

LUSTFUL LYRICS AND MACHO MOVIES

Whether you listen to golden oldies, nineties classics, or modern-day crooners, male singers never seem to miss an opportunity to share their insatiable desire to be with, or surrounded by, numerous women. They tell us implicitly, and sometimes *explicitly*, that their desire is so insatiable that *one* woman could never be enough. Think about the seemingly innocent Beach Boys swooning over the beautiful girls all over the world, wishing they *all* could live in California. Or, on the other end of the spectrum, Ludacris bragging about having "hoes" in different area codes. Or Shaggy having so many sexual encounters with women that he comes up with one ridiculous lie after another in hopes he doesn't get caught *repeatedly* cheating. And then there are the messages that suggest men's desire is surface level and purely physical in nature: Sir Mix-A-Lot fetishizing the female backside, Ed Sheeran obsessing over the shape of his crush's body, or Bruno Mars's love song about how "amazing" his female interest is, followed *exclusively* by examples of her physical beauty. And don't get me started on the go-to images of the male singer surrounded by countless scantily clad women as if he could never get enough of them to satisfy his strong sexual urges!

And that's just the tip of the iceberg. We also have a plethora of visual images of men in cinema who are on the hunt for sex and movies that make chasing women a central part of the plot. There are the stereotypical teen flicks where the guys are on a quest to lose their virginity (*American Pie*, *Superbad*, and *The Girl Next Door*, just to name a few) and the "cool" male characters who are always surrounded by women who are *oozing* sex (like James Bond, Don Draper, or Tony Soprano). And then there are movies that use a man's *lack* of interest in sex as fodder for laughter: think of *Horrible Bosses* and the ridicule Charlie Day's character receives when he says his female boss, played by the beautiful Jennifer Aniston, is sexually harassing him. His male friends say they *wish* she were harassing them. Because, what kind of a guy wouldn't want and happily accept *her* sexual offerings?

If there is any part of you that's thinking that these are silly, fun examples that we shouldn't take that seriously, I'll give you another example to show how deep-rooted this simplistic depiction of men's desire runs.

THIS IS (NOT) US

Full disclosure: my husband and I are obsessed with the show *This Is Us*. We get so invested that we can't handle watching just one episode at a time, so every other week we watch two taped episodes back-to-back with a glass of wine, and we laugh and tear up, and talk about how bang on the show is in terms of capturing these deep emotional joys and struggles we (and many others) face.

And, as much as it pains me to say this about my favorite show, I have to confess that between scenes of *epic* emotional proportions, I've noticed some narrow stereotypes about the male characters and their interest in sex.

OK, there. I said it.

Now that it's out there, I'll give you a couple of examples.

In one scene Randal and his wife, Beth, are having an argument in the bathroom. Then, instead of engaging in the conversation, Beth suggestively removes her bathrobe and Randal laughs off everything he had been upset about, the implication being that sex cures all—for men at least. Another time Toby was in the hospital after a heart attack. When Kate comes to visit him to make sure he's OK, he makes joke after joke about wanting her to climb on top of him so they can hook up on the hospital bed. After having a *heart attack*! As if there is literally *never* a time when a man wouldn't want to get laid.

It struck me as so profound that a show that gets *so much* right about our human complexities and emotional relationships *still* has these scenes that depict men as simple and sex hungry (and women as being less interested in sex). It goes without saying that if a show as nuanced and emotionally sophisticated as *This Is Us* projects simplified versions of men's sexuality, we are seeing it everywhere.

WHERE DOES THIS COME FROM?

Whatever the medium and however the message is being conveyed, these are not one-off here-and-there examples pulled out of thin air. We have received these sorts of messages consistently and *incessantly* over the course of our lives. Whether through stories, movies, music videos, or advertisements, the barrage seems to never end.

Maybe you noticed the stereotyped portrayals in these movies, scenes, and songs (or similar ones) and maybe you didn't. You would be forgiven for *not* noticing because these depictions are so common and these messages so pervasive that we can easily take them in without questioning what they are really suggesting about men and sex. It's just what we have become accustomed to—endless reminders that men's desire is (or *should* be) high, constant, unwavering, and simple.

There are several theories about how this came to be.

DO THE EVOLUTION

Imagine, if you will, *my* all-time favorite sitcom lovebirds: Jim and Pam. Just try to forget about this ridiculously cute couple's romantic life on *The Office* and pretend Jim and Pam's *only* goal is to produce offspring. Forget about the flirting, cute longing stares, air high-fives, and stolen kisses. Strip away all the emotions, love, connection, commitment, and basic human decency, and just think about what Jim and Pam *must* do in order to procreate.

First, Pam has to have sex with Jim. Then, should Pam get pregnant, the baby must live and grow inside her body for nine months (give or take). Then she has to *give birth to* the baby. And, after that, the infant is highly dependent on Pam for nursing and protection until the baby is old enough to fend for him- or herself. On top of all that, during Pam's pregnancy she is not able to get pregnant again. She is out of commission in terms of procreating for those nine months and then for a period of time after the baby is born while her body heals.

Now, Jim is a whole different story. Jim only *needs* to be present for the relatively brief sexual encounter that gets Pam pregnant, which at best is a longish romp (I'll be generous and say ten minutes, but statistically speaking it's most likely closer to two minutes).[1] Then, technically, Jim could just . . . leave. Never come back. Provided Pam carries the baby to term, his genes have been passed on. Not only that, if Jim *wanted* to, he could sleep with other women and try getting *them* pregnant in a quest to continue passing on his genes, baby by baby, with very little time or investment other than two minutes of thrusting and ejaculating.

I know, I know. This is obviously an *incredibly* simplified version of procreation in order to make a point. But it does highlight some realities that have existed for men and women for years and years before marriage and monogamy existed. According to some evolutionary theorists, women have evolved to desire sex in the context of a committed partnership, one in which she trusts that the male who got her pregnant will stick around during her pregnancy (and beyond) to help ensure the survival of her offspring (protecting the child from threats of danger, helping to provide food, and so on).[2] It's in her best interest and the interest of her baby to keep sex in this kind of partnership. So, no one-night stands, no sex with men who don't seem committed, and a discerning eye to avoid men who aren't going to stick around. Instead, women may have evolved to prefer romance, love, commitment, and security in order to feel amorous.

In contrast, some evolutionary theorists suggest that over a very, very, *very* long period of time, men evolved to experience *higher* levels of desire that could be triggered easily and often in order to avoid missing an opportunity to procreate with an available female. That means men's sexual desire may have evolved to be strong and constant, always right below the surface in case an opportunity suddenly presents itself. It would also benefit men to experience desire for many different women who are easily available, and when he perceives commitment levels to be low. In other words, men (at least theoretically) want to engage in casual sex with any female in any circumstance.[3]

Well maybe not *any* woman. In order to make procreation even *more* likely, it is theorized, male sexual desire is influenced by surface-level characteristics (i.e., attractive, young, healthy women with an hourglass shape), which may suggest a female is more likely to be fertile and that his chances of procreating are increased.[4]

MONKEY SEE, MONKEY DO

What I just outlined is a biologically and deep-rooted belief about potentially fundamental differences between men and women based on years and years and *years* of our species evolving. But there is another theory about men's sexual desire being high and unwavering that is quite different than this evolutionary theory. Some sociologists have suggested that rather than men's sexuality being something *innate*, our society shapes, rewards, and ultimately "grooms" men to demonstrate higher levels of interest in sexual activity.[5]

Social messages about what boys and girls "should" do start as early as the day we are born. We're all familiar with the tradition of dressing newborn girls in pink onesies (and newborn boys in blue) to make sure there is no mistaking that *this* Taylor is a girl Taylor who has a vagina (and not *that* Taylor who is a boy and has a penis). As we get older, boys tend to get trucks and camouflaged GI Joes, while girls tend to get frilly dresses and princess dolls. Boys are encouraged to be rough and tough (and not wimpy), girls to be polite and cooperative (and not bossy). And peppered throughout these social messages about what boys and girls wear, like, and do, there are also *plenty* of things we learn about our sexualities.

First, there is this issue of how boys and girls are "allowed" to touch themselves. Most adults are relatively uncomfortable when they first encounter their son or daughter touching their genitals in a way that elicits pleasure. But within this discomfort are noticeable differences in how parents react to their sons and daughters. That's because boys' penises are just *there*, outside of their bodies, easily viewed and easily stumbled upon as they learn to reach and grab. And as they get to an age where they go to the bathroom on their own, boys *need* to touch their penis in order to avoid peeing on the toilet seat, making the handling of their genitals completely commonplace, even necessary.[6]

Girls' genitals, on the other hand, are largely tucked inside their bodies. As a result, it often takes girls longer to stumble upon their vulvas, let alone their vaginas. And girls do not need to touch their genitals in order to do the practical chore of urinating. So touching their vulvas and vaginas becomes something that is almost solely for sexual pleasure. Which makes most adults *extremely* uncomfortable. So girls are more often scolded for touching their genitals. "Don't do that; it's dirty!" they are often told.

The messages about boys' and girls' sexuality only intensify once they hit puberty and throughout their teenage years and early adulthood. Young women are taught to avoid sexual encounters for fear of having an unwanted pregnancy or acquiring a sexually transmitted disease or infection. And health risks are only half of it. Women are also often shamed by society if they are sexually active at a young age and, even worse, if they are sexually promiscuous. Words like *slut* and *whore* are thrown around to shame and tame women into being sexually demure and reserved.[7]

Young men, on the other hand, don't tend to receive the same warnings about sex. They might be taught that they should use a condom when they have sex but usually not to avoid sex altogether; in fact, quite the opposite: men are often encouraged to push to the next level of sexual intimacy and rewarded (through admiration, popularity, and social status) for having sex with one or (even better) multiple sexual partners.

Ultimately, some sociologists suggest that men are encouraged to embrace their desires and act upon them, while women learn to repress their sexual feelings. Men are taught to initiate sexual activity, to desire sex (not to be desirable), to push to the next level of physical intimacy, and to be highly sexually skilled in order to impress their female partner. Sociologists have also suggested that men are encouraged to prefer recreational or casual sex, to value sex as simply an act rather than a means to a relationship, to want no-strings-attached sex, and to seek out multiple partners.[8]

So, it may not be that men and women have drastically different levels of desire to *start* with. But over time, women are taught to repress their desires, while men are encouraged to embrace them. Although this theory suggests that we *learn* to demonstrate our sexual desire in certain ways, it similarly concludes that men's desire is—or perhaps more accurately, *should* be—high, constant, and unwavering.

BE A MAN

Messages about men's sexual desire are even further complicated by the concept of masculinity. Sigh . . . *that* word. *Masculinity*. What was once simply a neutral term to convey qualities that were associated with being a man is now a loaded term that can pressure and confine men to abide by a certain male code of conduct. To prove that they are the most manly of all men. All. The. Time.[9]

The key thing to being masculine is, well, essentially not being perceived as feminine. The pursuit of masculinity (or perhaps more accurately, "toxic masculinity") is said to include everything from being aggressive, to suppressing one's emotions, to distancing oneself from other men, to striving for competition, success, and power.[10] And then there is sex.

Do you know what happens to be stereotypically considered "feminine" with regard to sex? Having *low* desire. So, what does being manly look like with regard to sexual desire? It means the antithesis of low desire. A "real man" would never have a low interest in sex. He would never turn down a sexual opportunity. He would never *not* be ready for sex at the drop of a hat because a real man is always thinking about sex. Because failing to initiate sexual activity or show a strong interest in sex can call into question a man's masculinity and even his sexual orientation.[11]

Sex within the context of masculinity theory also means being interested in having sex with multiple women, as sexual inexperience is stigmatized. Men with multiple partners or an in-depth knowing of women continue to be revered over the guy who doesn't date or doesn't sleep around. And stereotypically masculine sex *also* means pushing to the next level of sexual intimacy. Initiating sex in a relationship. Pursuing women in dating contexts. Asking again even when the answer is no (I don't have to point out how toxic *that* is). And it means desiring women without being an object of desire oneself. *I want* you*; I don't need you to want me. You are the object of my desire, not the other way around.*

I will offer a criticism of how this limited (yet pervasive) belief about masculinity is harming men's and women's intimate relationships when we get to the *masculinity myth.* For now, I will simply say that the current traditional ideal of masculinity exists in spades and plays a large role in how many men feel they are supposed to experience and demonstrate their interest in sex.

MEN AND SEX 101: A SUMMARY

No matter where we turn we are exposed to the notion that men's sexual desire is high, constant, and relatively surface level.

- Stereotypes about men's desire being high and unwavering are reinforced over and over through TV shows, movies, advertisements, and song lyrics, just to name a few.
- Evolutionary theorists suggest that men have evolved to experience higher interest in sex to procreate with multiple females and never miss a sexual opportunity, thereby increasing their chances of passing on their genes.
- According to evolutionary theory, men would therefore be attracted to surface-level physical characteristics that help them determine if a woman is fertile and be less interested in committed, partnered sex.

- Sexual script theorists suggest that rather than sexual desire being innate, men have been encouraged by society to embrace their sexuality and act upon their sexual urges.
- Society is thought to have "groomed" men into being more comfortable initiating sex, doing the desiring, and taking any sexual opportunity presented to them.
- Masculinity theorists suggest that men experience pressure to prove their masculinity over and over by demonstrating an omnipresent interest in sex and never saying no to sexual opportunities.

Taken collectively, we are left with the following beliefs about men and sex:

- Men's sexual desire is high and unwavering.
- Men have higher sex drives than women.
- Men's sexual desire is largely triggered by surface-level physical cues.
- Men are primarily motivated by their own sexual gratification.
- Pornography is integral to men's sex lives.
- Men do the desiring; they don't need to feel desirable themselves.
- Men pursue and initiate all sexual activity.
- Sexual rejection doesn't hurt; men are used to it and expect it.
- Men will take any sexual opportunity that comes their way.
- Real men are comfortable playing by these rules.

Now that we know where these pillars about men and sex come from, let's start tearing them down, shall we?

MYTH I

The Motivation Myth

"I don't know what's wrong with me."

This was practically Patrick's therapy mantra, the phrase he repeated over and over again as we talked, as if in a trance.

"My wife is beautiful. I'm still attracted to her. And I *should* want to have sex with her, but I'm just not interested. I don't know what's wrong with me—I just don't feel like myself these days."

Patrick had initially come to see me about difficulties he was having while adjusting to several changes in his life. He had just started a new job with his family business and felt an incredible amount of pressure to successfully carry on his father's legacy. He and his wife had a new baby at home. He turned forty last year. There were bills to pay: mortgage, cell phones, cable, Internet, two cars. There were trips that they wanted to take but couldn't afford. They had a beloved dog that was getting older and sicker.

Patrick was fairly receptive to how these changes were having a negative impact on his emotional well-being. And he was open to discussions about self-care to mitigate the stress. However, he had a harder time recognizing that these same factors could be explaining the decrease in his sexual interest.

"I'm forty years old—not a geriatric! I should be able to handle this stress. Everyone my age has a job, and bills, and kids. Sex used to make me feel relaxed," he said, flabbergasted. "Now it just feels like one more thing I have to do." Followed by the predictable, "Seriously, what's *wrong* with me?"

* * *

Over the course of this book we will delve deeper and deeper into men's sexual desire, highlighting the nuanced and often overlooked complexities of men's sexual experiences. But I want to start by challenging the widely held myth that ties together all of the forthcoming chapters: the overarching belief that men's sexual desire is high. Period. The myth that implies men's desire starts high and *stays* high. The myth that men's desire is somehow impermeable to what happens outside of the bedroom. The myth that men want sex anytime, anyplace, anywhere, no matter what.

Specifically, we will focus on how there were *several* reasons Patrick had a decreased interest in sex: from his age, to work stress, to the mounting responsibilities he was facing. And that the negative impact these factors were having on his sexual desire was normal, natural, and far more common among men than many of us tend to recognize.

MY FIFTEEN MINUTES OF FAME

Early in my research career, I published a study that found that while women experienced a steady decrease in sexual desire over the course of their long-term relationships, men's desire stayed the same regardless of whether they had been in their relationship for one month or ten years.[1] In other words, the findings suggested that unlike women, men's desire remained high and fairly constant over the course of a long-term relationship.

The findings were published in national newspapers like the *Globe and Mail* and psychology blogs like *Live Science* and, to my surprise, were even fodder for conversation on *Regis and Kelly* (when Regis was still in the business—like I said, this was early in my career!). Although it was thrilling to have my research publicly recognized, the experience of having months of research condensed into a media sound bite had me questioning how the message was being conveyed.

Here's why: I just gave you the gist of my findings—what the media shared. That men's desire stays high while women's desire decreases over the course of a relationship. But here is an additional, very crucial detail. The sample of this study? University students aged eighteen to twenty-five years old.

If that doesn't immediately strike you as important, here's why it is. If you've ever taken a first-year university class, you know that this is the primary sampling pool researchers use to recruit for their studies. But it hardly allows us to extrapolate and say that this finding would continue *past* the age range we used. And while any respectable researcher will note these comments in the limitations section of his or her research papers (and I can assure you, we most certainly did!), these limitations and considerations are hardly ever shared alongside the findings in the media. Or, if they are, they are buried down behind a catchier headline.

Here is why that matters: men in my study were still young. *Really* young. They were all relatively healthy. They were in university. Only a small minority (less than 5 percent) were married. And none of them had kids. The reality, as anyone over the age of twenty-five knows all too well, is this: when you look a few years down the road, many of these variables change. So what we absolutely cannot, I repeat *cannot*, conclude from this study is that men's desire stays high *past* twenty-five years old. *Or* that men's desire remains high over the course of a long-term relationship after age twenty-five.

And what happens beyond age twenty-five is hugely important because (a) the vast majority of the adult population is older than twenty-five, and (b) being over twenty-five is associated with a whole slew of life changes that are found to impact sexual desire.

So let's explore those over-the-twenty-five-year-old-hill variables: getting older, the associated responsibilities, and, finally, the impact of being in a longer-term relationship.

NOT WHAT IT USED TO BE

"Well, it's sure not what it used to be . . . ," followed by an awkward laugh. A somewhat casual brush-off. And, most likely, a furtive glance to see how I react.

I've seen it more times than I can count: men walk into my office or speak to me during research interviews and start to open up about how their desire is no longer pulsating out of their bodies. How they don't want to jump their wives every second of every day. How perhaps they *used* to think about sex "constantly" or wanted sex whenever they could get it, but recently they are more interested in a movie, a beer, and an earlier bedtime.

In fact, there seems to be an acknowledgment that the stereotypically young man with high sexual desire is, well, a *young* man. But what is "young" exactly?

When we think about men first having a high interest in sex, we're really talking about boys *on the verge* of becoming men. In other words, when they hit puberty. In modern Western countries, puberty occurs on average between twelve and fourteen years old (of course, there are exceptions to this rule with some men hitting puberty earlier or later than this).[2] When men hit puberty, their testosterone levels peak. These higher levels of testosterone have several notable impacts, from the appearance of acne to the broadening of shoulders to a pretty intense sexual interest. And that's because sexual desire is connected to the amount of testosterone pulsating through men's bodies. In other words, during puberty the floodgates of testosterone open and desire spikes. The Netflix show *Big Mouth* offers an entertaining example of how men's sexual interest is experienced at this age. It's depicted as an almost compulsive and impulsive urge to masturbate, to find anything (and everything) sexual, and to get erections left, right, and center.

These spiked levels of testosterone are found to remain fairly high and constant in puberty and throughout young men's teenage years. But what happens *after* that?

From a biological standpoint testosterone levels tend to, on average, remain high until about age thirty and then start decreasing ever so slightly there on out.[3] Studies offer different takes on exactly how much testosterone drops and when, but generally speaking it seems to follow the general age progression that mirrors retirement and senior citizenship. In other words, once men hit sixty-five years old, a decreased interest in sex is seen as natural and normal (and socially accepted).

This decrease in sexual desire around sixty-five even has a name: andropause. The term *andropause*—literally named for the "pause" in the production of androgens (which include testosterone)—was developed to document the changes men's bodies go through when they experience a more dramatic drop in testosterone levels. When a man's androgens and testosterone levels significantly decrease, his energy level goes down, his strength decreases, and—more often than not—so does his sex drive.

Older age (again, roughly sixty-five years and older) is also associated with increased rates of illness, which tend to negatively impact sexual desire.[4] For example, prostate cancer and diabetes are more likely to occur later on in life and are associated with lower sexual desire in men.

Chances are that a lot of you reading this book are likely *under* sixty-five years old. So you might be thinking, "OK, so men's sexual desire decreases later on in life. Perhaps years or even decades from now. But what about *now*?"

Well, as briefly mentioned before, testosterone levels *start* dropping around thirty, which means men's sexual desire might start to change around this time and moving forward. The other thing? Hormones are far from the only factor at play as we age.

THE EVERGREEN MALE TEENAGER

So far I've been talking about biological changes in men's testosterone levels and how those changes impact men's sexual interest. But what I've come to see throughout my career is that men's *interpretations* of the changes to their bodies don't always follow so nicely along this biological line.

That is, in *addition* to the natural biological changes occurring in men's testosterone levels as they get older, men's interpretations of their changing desire also impact their sexual experiences. Just because we have documented trends about sexual desire decreasing around sixty-five doesn't mean that *all* men have high sexual urges up until that point. In fact, over the course of my interviews with men, it seems that men in their late thirties and early forties are the ones who identified being most aware of (and sometimes the most *distressed* about) their desire not being what it used to be. And it's my observation that this is because that decreased interest in sex happened a lot earlier than they were expecting.

Here are a few of the men I spoke with—well below the age of sixty-five—describing the changes they noticed in their sexual desire over time:

> "I think as you get older you have less desire" (Jeffrey, age forty-three).

"I never ever thought I would lose that desire, but it really, it's . . . I'm losing that desire. It's just not that interesting to me anymore" (Daniel, age thirty-eight).

"For a long period of time in my life, [sexual desire] appeared to be very strong. For the last while it's reducing" (William, age forty-six).

"I'm forty now and I would say in the last couple years I have noticed the urgency has dropped off for sure. Which is maybe a little depressing, but it's happening so what can you do? But when I was definitely younger and I would say up to thirty-five, the desire would still be a daily occurrence, even a couple of times a day. Now I can go two or three days and it's whatever. It has nothing to do with my wife and her attractiveness or anything . . . I think it's just getting older" (Brian, age forty).

Men's perspectives of when their desire changes are important. If we hold the idea that men "should" have high desire until they are older (again I'll use that sixty-five-year-old cutoff to be consistent with the majority of studies in the field), when men in their thirties, forties, and fifties naturally feel their sexual desire is decreasing, they can be more troubled by it—partially because they think they shouldn't have a decreased desire. Not *yet* at least.

However, it seems to be fairly common that starting in their thirties, men may start noticing a drop in their sexual desire levels. And the adjustment to these changes is worthy of some attention. Because while testosterone production still is, on average, relatively high at this point, men in their thirties and forties also have a heap of other factors impacting their desire.

CARTWHEELS TURN TO CAR WHEELS

There are plenty of life events that negatively impact men's desire and occur alongside getting older. Perhaps the biggest one? Having children.

Although I certainly work with clients in their late teens and twenties, the majority of people I work with and interview are thirty years old and above. And that tends to mean many are parents. I think all women who have kids know that being a mother, and especially being a *new* mother, can have a significant impact on their sexuality. Women's bodies have to recover from pregnancy and child delivery, and their focus moves from "all about me" to taking care of a little person (or *persons*). Not to mention a number of female body parts that used to be sexualized (like vaginas and nipples) have shifted into being *functional*. Mentally this can be a bit of a difficult gap to bridge for women when it comes to sex. And did I mention the endless sleepless nights?

Socially speaking we have come a long way in terms of men's involvement as they enter their role as dad. Long gone are the days of Don Draper where fathers smoked cigars in the waiting room while their wife gave birth to their baby. Now dads are the most likely companion in the delivery room, holding their wives' hands while she groans, screams, and pushes. Dads are also increasingly helping with bedtime routines, taking kids to piano lessons, picking them up after school, and more. (On a personal note, my husband and I recently took our daughter to her first swimming class and noted that of the twelve parents in the pool with their kids, eleven of them were dads.)

Are mothers still doing the brunt of the child-rearing workload? In many homes the answer is yes. But most men aren't sitting over on the sidelines feeling little to no impact from being a father. In fact, being a father can have a significant, and negative, influence on men's sexual interest. And many of the men I've talked with have described various ways that having children negatively impacted their sexual desire. For example, one man I spoke with, a father of three, described that having children consumed a lot of time and left little room for himself and his relationship:

> "Having one child: challenge. Having two: bigger challenge, right? It's challenging enough to raise two kids, but at least there is one of us for each child. But you add a third one, and now we're totally outnumbered. Always. Which means at any point somebody isn't getting what they need. And then how do you find time for yourself? When you've added that much more responsibility to your life."

It's not just the demands of having children that negatively impact men's desire. But cognitively, just knowing that children are around can be a sex buzz kill for men. There is not a lot of alone time, there is little privacy, and you never know when you're going to be interrupted or walked in on. For example, one of my participants, Justin, said the uncertainty about having privacy during a sexual encounter when his children were home killed his sexual desire. He indicated that the thought of them walking in and seeing him in the middle of a sexual act was too big of a risk and reduced his desire altogether—even though his wife did not necessarily hold those same worries:

> "Sometimes on a Saturday or whatever, my wife will get frisky and she'll want to sneak away and do it. And, you know, as soon as I hear one of the kids, I lose all desire . . . because of them coming in or them interrupting. The idea of that horrifies me."

Having kids can also have an *indirect* impact on men's desire. That is, some men find that while *they* could put their worries aside and focus on sex, their female partner has become much more focused on their children. As a result some men feel that they have fallen to the back burner. In fact, it's not at all uncommon for men to note a qualitative difference in their sexual satisfaction post children and to describe a decreased sexual desire because they felt their female partner had lost interest in sex. Just listen to John recalling that after the kids were born, his wife's focus turned away from him and sex and toward the children; consequently, he felt his sexual desire wane:

> "My partner wanted the kids more than I did. And it has been a challenge in that, I guess, I really enjoyed the physical part of the relationship very much at first. And as the kids come along, her focus shifted to the kids and, I felt, away from me. And the fun in many ways of life, including sexually, went down considerably."

How interested women are in having sex with their male partner has a *huge* impact on men's sexual interest. When men's partners are tired, distracted, or not feeling very sexy or sexual, men's own sexual interest often decreases as well. (We'll dive into *much* more detail on that dynamic once we get to the *selfish myth*.)

ADULTING IS HARD

Do you remember when the extent of your responsibilities and decision making was whether you studied enough for your exams to warrant going out again that night?

I'm not saying that school wasn't somewhat stressful. But as we know all too well, the older we get, the more and more responsibilities pile on. Maybe we get a pet. Or we start paying a mortgage instead of rent—or at least we start paying more expensive rent on our own or with a partner instead of split between five roommates. We get a car. We have a job. We need to pay more bills. And those mounting responsibilities impact us on multiple levels—including our sexual desire.

And I'll let you in on a little secret: men's desire isn't impermeable to these heightened responsibilities.

I've spoken with many men who have highlighted how having so many things just piling up so high and wide makes them feel as though there is no time to experience sexual desire. They say that they don't have time to nurture or embrace their sexual interest when a million other things are demanding their attention first. Here are just a few examples:

"We age, we have children, we have responsibilities, so there are other things that kick in. And that desire doesn't disappear; it's just subdued a little bit."

"Usually when there is no desire is usually when I have a lot of other stuff in front of me. And it could be it's twenty after five, I've got to grab some supper and then I have class at six. And my son's just gone to the bathroom on the toilet and needs me to come wipe his bum and my other son is . . . you know? So when there is no desire it is usually because there is a whole lot of other stuff that is stacked up in front of me preventing me from getting there."

"If you get too focused on what you have to do to get through the day—like make sure you've got the meals organized, get to work, do what you have to do, things like that—that you start to put everything immediate in getting in the day ahead of things that make you feel the pleasant desire and romance type feelings that you can start not noticing them. Sort of like you're not having them anymore."

The interesting thing about these quotes is that men aren't necessarily saying that their desire is gone forever. They seem to identify that it's there somewhere. That they feel urges or interests at times but are just so busy, so tired, or so tied up with a million other things that have to come first that sexual desire just dampens. And it seems that feeling stressed about those to-dos has the strongest impact on men's desire. A few other men put this experience in their own words:

> "Now that we're busier, with jobs and stuff, a little more stress comes with that. And there is no doubt in my mind, I am sure stress dampens desire."

> "I've noticed at some points in my life if I'm really stressed, that is gone. There is no sexual desire. It's not like anything's missing. It's just not where my mind is at."

> "The older I get, especially at night before I go to bed, I get these thoughts that I'm getting older. I'm thirty-eight and there is a lot of stress. Did I accomplish everything I needed to accomplish? That's a lot in my head now."

These quotes highlight that while we may think of sex as being a way to relax (and it certainly can be for some folks), it's important to acknowledge that mounting responsibilities can also be a sex buzz kill for some men. And that when men are feeling overwhelmed and burdened by their to-do lists, sometimes sex simply isn't on their radar.

LOVERS BECOME FRIENDS

Think about your romantic partner for a minute. Would you say that you possess a *powerful* attraction to them? Would you say you can't control your thoughts because they are *obsessively* on that person? That you have an *endless* appetite for affection from them?

If you're thinking, "Um . . . no, not really" or "I guess? A little bit? Sometimes?" Don't worry!

These are items from a scale that Drs. Elaine Hatfield and Susan Sprecher developed to measure passionate love.[5] Passionate love is theorized to occur at the very early stages of a relationship. And the beginning of the relationship tends to be full of erotic passion.[6] We are almost *obsessed* with our partners. We want to spend all of our time with them and even when they aren't with us we are thinking about them constantly. It's almost like falling in love gives you super powers. You can stay up late and run off little sleep as long as you're talking with your boo. And sexual desire is thought to be quite high and rampant at this stage too. In pop culture we refer to this time as the honeymoon phase (even though for most couples today it occurs long before any honeymoon!).

But as anyone who has ever been in a relationship for more than a few months knows, the way things feel *now* is likely quite different compared to how our relationship felt at the beginning. Over time, we start to notice a decrease in that passion. We start to realize that maybe we should go to bed so we don't feel so tired for our early morning meeting. We reconnect with friends we have been neglecting. We make time to go to the gym again. And our partner, as we get to know them better and better, becomes a friend. We can still feel desire for them. There can still be moments of passion. But the lust that distracted us from all other parts of our lives subsides, and a calmer friendship of sorts takes its place.

These feelings comprise the following stage of a relationship, known as companionate love. Companionate love, as the name suggests, highlights the change in relationship feelings where our partner feels a bit more like a *companion*, not just our sexual partner. If you are experiencing companionate love, you might be more likely to agree with statements that highlight your long-term commitment and attachment to your partner, such as "I am committed to maintaining my relationship with _____," "I have confidence in the stability of my relationship with _____," and "_____ is able to count on me in times of need."[7]

And that *is normal and healthy*. In fact, we almost have to shift out of permanent passionate love in order to survive. Think about what would happen if ten years into your relationship you still were acting the way you did in the first few week and months of dating. You likely wouldn't have many friends, your work would be suffering, and you certainly wouldn't have the time or energy to devote to kids (should that be part of your plan).

So, when many of us think about men's sexual desire being high and unwavering, we are failing to recognize that desire naturally changes and decreases over the course of a relationship. And, given that most of our population, particularly most of our population above thirty years old, are *in* longer-term relationships, we need to remember this is a life factor that affects women *and* men. And that changes in men's sexual desire over time are natural and normal, not something to be pathologized.

"PROBLEMATIC" LOW SEXUAL DESIRE

When we think of terms like *low libido* or *low sexual desire*, our minds more often than not focus on women. And for good reason—there are plenty of women who experience problematic low sexual desire.

What exactly is "problematic low sexual desire"? It can be a little difficult to pin down because different researchers have been using different criteria to measure and study this phenomenon.[8] However, generally speaking this term is used to describe the experience of low sexual desire that causes the person some level of distress over an extended period of time. How long and how distressing is what is left up to interpretation (although it is worth noting that the latest version of the *Diagnostic and Statistical Manual of Mental Disorders*—a.k.a. the mental health bible— uses the criteria that low desire must be present and distressing for at least six months and 75 to 100 percent of the time for it to be diagnosed as hypoactive sexual interest/arousal disorder).[9]

It's important for us to better understand problematic low sexual desire in women as this is a very common experience that causes a great deal of distress for many women. Research regularly and reliably finds that 30 percent of women experience what used to be called hypoactive sexual desire disorder (desire so low that they are emotionally distressed).[10]

In contrast there is less data on how many men experience low sexual desire. The results from epidemiological studies on low sexual desire vary considerably; however, the trend that relatively fewer men (when compared to women) report low sexual desire is consistent. The number of men who report problematic low sexual desire fluctuates depending on definition and criteria used by researchers. For example, when asked whether they had experienced a "distressing loss of sexual desire" over the last twelve months, 8 percent of Norwegian men aged twenty-two to sixty-seven indicated that they did either "all the time," "nearly all the time," or "quite often."[11] Whereas in a national health study of American men, researchers determined that 15 percent of the male population between the ages of eighteen and fifty-nine had "persistent complaints of low sexual desire."[12]

Although these two studies suggest there could be a range of men who experience problematic low sexual desire, a summary article exploring the prevalence rates of low sexual desire across several studies and countries reported that approximately 14 to 19 percent of men regularly and reliably indicated that they experienced problematically low or decreased sexual desire.[13] Taking these findings together, one could conclude that approximately one in ten to almost one in five men experience problematic low sexual desire at any point in time.

However, what I will say once here and will repeat over and over again in some way, shape, or form throughout this book is that when we focus on gender differences, we can miss some of the nuances that both women and men experience. Specifically, while we regularly see headlines such as "Twice as many women as men experience low sexual desire"—which is completely true—what we focus on is that many women experience low sexual desire and ignore that 15 percent of men do as well.

That is, since women are found to experience problematic low sexual desire more often than men, men seem to have been left out of the research. Consequently we know relatively little about men's experiences and what leads to problematic low sexual desire. However, here is what we do know: men who report problematic or distressing low sexual desire often cite medical and biological reasons as responsible, such as certain medications (e.g., some antidepressants) or the aftermath of a serious medical illness and/or surgery (e.g., prostate cancer). In the study of Norwegian men mentioned earlier, men's third most commonly cited reason for low sexual interest was "diseases." And in the American study described earlier, "health difficulties" was cited as one of the two most commonly reported issues leading to distressing low desire. Problematic low sexual desire is also regularly found to be an adaptive response to other male sexual problems, such as erectile dysfunction or premature ejaculation.

But as we explored earlier, men's sexual desire is also impacted by social, relational, and other contextual factors such as parenting and marital or work stress. These stresses can, and do, play a crucial role in decreased sexual interest: in one study, men indicated stress was the most likely reason for their distressing decreased interest in sex, even above health issues and diseases.[14] Other factors associated with problematic low sexual desire in men include restrictive attitudes toward sexuality, a lack of erotic thoughts during sexual encounters, concerns about erections, sadness, shame, or a history of sexual trauma.

So it should be clear that some men certainly do experience low sexual desire concerns. And that while *more* women experience problematic low desire, it is still a common experience among men as well.

WHY THIS MYTH IS A PROBLEM

Our society is *obsessed* with youth. Women are held to beauty standards that fixate on characteristics of the young and healthy. Perky breasts and butts; smooth, tight skin with no wrinkles; full heads of thick and luxurious—*anything* but gray—hair. And while men often get a free pass on appearances as they age (think about the "silver fox" and the "dad bod"), they don't necessarily get a pass on sexual virility. But it may be that men are the ones who care more about their changing interest than do their female counterparts.

Let me quickly tell you about one of my favorite studies. Researchers in New Zealand were interested in the experience of the *women* whose male partners took Viagra.[15] While men in the study said they wanted to have rock-hard erections to continue having good sex as they aged, women said they didn't necessarily like when their male partner took the "little blue pill." In fact, some women in the study said they enjoyed that their male partner had a slightly *softer* erection as they aged. That as their bodies changed, their partner's rock-hard erection was actually kind of painful. And that they wanted their sexual repertoire to focus more on the "outer course" touch, caressing, kissing, massaging, and oral sex. Things that he didn't need an erection for!

While this study was about erections and not desire per se, it highlights an important piece: sometimes men tend to want to hold on to a part of their sexuality that was more indicative of their teenage and early adulthood years, but their female partner may not care about that part even close to as much as they do.

Women: If your male partner has low sexual interest, your reaction may fall into one of two camps. The first is concern. The second is relief. I'll speak to each in turn.

If you find yourself concerned about your male partner's gradual or sudden decrease in sexual interest and you're in your thirties, forties, or fifties, hopefully it is helpful to know that this is not entirely uncommon. As we know from the research, about 15 percent of men have problematic low sexual desire. And that doesn't even include the men who have a lower or decreased interest in sex who don't report that this decrease is particularly distressing. So although we don't talk a lot about men with low desire, it happens, it's common, and it doesn't necessarily mean anything is terribly wrong with him, with you, or with your relationship. As we have explored in this chapter, decreased sexual desire for men is incredibly common in longer-term relationships and as men age.

That being said, men's decreased sexual desire *can* point to some other issues that may need addressing, like high stress, illness, and physical health concerns. If you're concerned about your male partner's lower sexual interest, it may be helpful to explore these areas in your and your partner's life to figure out whether attention outside of the bedroom could help with your sex life. For example, if your partner is experiencing a high level of stress or work overload, it may be helpful to talk and brainstorm potential solutions and find ways to relax. Can he step away from one of his extracurricular activities? Does that kitchen renovation need to happen this year? Can you cancel that gathering with your friends and just stay in to watch movies all weekend? You may find that focusing directly on stress reduction might indirectly help his interest in sex if that's what you're looking to achieve.

Then there is the second camp of women—those of you who perhaps considered your male partner's sexual desire too high in the past and are somewhat relieved that he has a decreased interest now. If your experience falls more into this category—congratulations! You may bask in the glow of more aligned sexual desire and possibly even higher sexual satisfaction.

But even though you're OK with it, you may find that your partner isn't. That's because a lot of men still tend to place a lot of pressure on themselves to experience high sexual desire. He may be feeling weird that his desire has decreased (over the course of this book we will explore the many ways this can take shape, from feigning an interest in sex to avoiding intimacy altogether). If your partner has a really high level of interest and it starts to drop off, maybe find a way of sharing that this new sexual interest feels more compatible and satisfying for you. Your partner might be worried about his changes and could benefit from knowing that you're OK with it.

Men: First things first—know that men's sexual desire is hardly a constant. It will naturally change as you age, the longer you're in a relationship, and depending on other changes in your life, from illness to stress to having children, just to name a few. If you are feeling the weight of these issues on your shoulders, the best thing to do is share your concerns with your partner. You don't have to go it alone. And more often than not, your partner will feel closer and more connected when you open up about your inner world and you stand a better chance of connecting authentically. If you need to reduce your stress level, figure out if there is something that can be taken off your to-do list. If you think there could be a medical concern, talk to your doctor.

But also ask yourself what your "gold standard" is with regard to your perceptions of sexual desire. Is sexual desire *allowed* to change over time? Do your ideas of when and how men's desire changes impact your beliefs about yourself? How are these stereotypes and norms impacting your self-perceptions? If there were no expectations about how much desire you *should* have, would you feel OK with what you're experiencing?

Along those lines, ask yourself whether your changing levels of desire is a problem for your partner, or if it's just a problem for you. You may be concerned about your decrease in desire, but she may be perfectly fine with the changes and see them as natural and normal. If you alone are stressed because of an internalized idea of how sexual desire is inextricably linked to what it means to be a man, I'll invite you to gently challenge that thinking.

MYTH IN ACTION: PATRICK

The Case of the Peter Pan Syndrome

Patrick was one of my first clients ever. I didn't know it at the time, but looking back it is clear how much our work together shaped my approach to therapy, my research, and my general outlook on men and sex.

Patrick had just turned forty. He had recently switched careers. His aging father wanted to pass on his family business. Patrick hadn't originally thought he would work for the family company, but as time passed it made sense for him to take over and try to carry the torch for his father's business legacy. He wanted to make a good impression at work. But he was stressed. Really, really stressed. He said he was worked up about having to make cold calls to increase his business, and he was really struggling to do it. Would the person want to work with him? Or would they take a pass now that his father was no longer in charge? What if he couldn't secure their business and his company fell apart? What if his dad was the only one who could really make this business work? Patrick said he started avoiding the phone, having panic attacks on days when he had to call business owners or make visits to their shops.

We started to work on managing his stress. We explored his fears about wanting to prove himself and provide for his family. We developed some concrete steps (relaxation techniques, realistic targets to hit, safe places outside of therapy to work through his fears). And this allowed him to make those cold calls a little more comfortably. It was as good an outcome as we could have hoped for, or so it seemed.

But after we got the stress under control, Patrick surprised me by calling to make another appointment. I remember being confused as we had agreed to short-term therapy and it seemed we had wrapped up our work. What else did he wish to talk about? Well, it turns out the work stress was important to work through; however, once it was addressed he could no longer ignore the relationship and sex issues that had crept to the surface.

Patrick squirmed and twitched on his chair and was clearly reluctant to say what brought him back to my office. But eventually he came out with it: he just wasn't interested in sex. He said he and his wife weren't having sex that often and when they did it wasn't all that great. He wasn't sure what was going on and felt weird even having said it out loud. He had always thought of himself as a sexual guy. Not the kind of guy who went two (three or even four) weeks without sex—and actually felt *OK* with it. And the fact he was forty was a big part of the problem. He said he still felt young. Young enough to still want sex at least!

Over the course of our session Patrick confessed that his low libido was actually the reason he had originally come to see me—but that the work stress was just easier to talk about. He wasn't even sure whether he was going to open up about the sex stuff at all. He had ideas about men not talking about that kind of thing.

Patrick was the perfect candidate for some psycho-education. Instead of delving deep into his childhood or messages he received about sex and other well-below-the-surface questions, we focused on providing some information that would put his circumstances into perspective. We talked about how stress from work was impacting his sexual interest—and that this *made sense*. How a baby at home completely changes the sexual intimacy between couples—and that this was normal. How men in their forties are no strangers to decreased sexual interest. How feeling the weight of the world on his shoulders but still expecting himself to perform as usual in the bedroom was nothing short of unrealistic.

Because the thing is, we can't always change the circumstances that are causing low desire. Patrick couldn't change his age, the fact he has a baby, or his career path (at least not for some time). But he could change his perspective of how these factors impacted his desire. And he could reduce some of the unnecessary pressure and burden he had been placing on his shoulders based on the fear and shame that he *shouldn't* feel less interested in sex.

SUMMARY

It should go without saying: men are humans, not robots. Men's sexual desire is not a static trait that never changes and is impermeable to outside influences. There are numerous reasons men might experience a decreased interest in sex, either long term or circumstantially.

- Men's sexual desire generally peaks at puberty when testosterone levels spike. These high levels of desire and testosterone remain throughout adolescence and into early adulthood.
- Sexual desire tends to decrease ever so slightly as men age, with a drop in testosterone levels occurring somewhere around thirty years old and a bigger decrease in testosterone occurring in late middle age (sometimes known as andropause).
- Many men in their thirties and forties may feel their desire is no longer what it used to be, as youthful teenage years are often used as an unrealistic point of comparison.

- Men who experience changes in desire earlier in life can often be the most distressed, as the social discourse about men's desire being high and constant is dominant and pervasive.
- Men's sexual interest is not impervious to social and relational dynamics. Some of the biggest changes that impact desire include the introduction of children and stress from increasing adult responsibilities.
- While passion and desire are possible at all stages of a relationship, it is common for women *and* men in longer-term relationships to feel less desire for their partner as their relationship becomes long term.
- About 15 percent of men across studies report problematically low sexual desire that may qualify as diagnosable and treatable.

MYTH 2

The Gender Myth

"I can't get it up."

They were the first words Jarrod spoke when he and Anna sat down in my office. Jarrod was a straight shooter who wanted to get right down to the matter at hand. He wanted to understand why he had difficulties getting an erection and how to fix it. Yesterday, if possible.

"He's got a problem. I don't know what it's about, but it had better get resolved soon," Anna echoed. Anna was Jarrod's girlfriend of about five years and she seemed to be just as distraught as Jarrod, perhaps even more so, about the issue. She wanted to have sex, and more often than not he couldn't get or maintain an erection long enough to do so. And it had been happening for over a year now.

Jarrod was a healthy guy. He worked out and took care of himself. He focused on what he ate and what he drank. And he was in his thirties. Not quite the description that first comes to mind when we think about the typical makeup of someone experiencing erectile difficulties.

But as we continued our conversation it became clear that Jarrod's erectile difficulties were not so much a physical issue. After all, he could get erections on his own while masturbating, spontaneously in the morning, and *sometimes* when he and Anna wanted to have sex. But there were more and more times when Anna wanted to have sex and Jarrod's body simply didn't respond.

And it was *supposed* to. Because, when it comes to men and women, it's the guy who is always interested in having sex . . . right?

* * *

Throughout this chapter we'll continue to challenge the idea of men's sexual desire being high, constant, and unwavering. Specifically, we will focus on how assumptions we make about men's desire are often a direct comparison to assumptions we make about women's desire. In other words, we tend to consider men's desire as *high*, meaning high*er* and more constant than women's desire. And when it's not—when a woman wants sex and her male partner doesn't—a slew of problems can show up in heterosexual relationships.

HIGHER THAN WHAT?

To make the statement that men are more interested in sex than women are is painting with a pretty broad stroke. And with any statement of that magnitude there are going to be some exceptions to the rule. It's like saying men tend to be taller than women, but then citing examples that run counter to that fact, like Maria Sharapova or Danny DeVito.

So when it comes to sex, you may know a guy who has never really seemed *that* into sex. The kind of guy who stayed pretty quiet during conversations about sex or never really made "hooking up" as much of a priority as the rest of the group back in your single days. On the other hand, perhaps you know a woman who is explicitly open and comfortable with her sexuality, or proudly shares her sexcapades when you're out having drinks.

In other words, when we make such large, generalized statements, it is hard to imagine anyone not having an example of *someone* who doesn't seem to fit this norm.

But I am talking beyond the exception-to-the-rule heuristic. From the research and my clinical experience, I can say that there are so many exceptions to this "rule" that I suggest the proposed "fact" that men have higher desire than women is, well, a myth.

MEN ARE FROM MARS

Treating men and women as separate entities with regard to sex and sexuality occurs everywhere, from pop culture magazines to living room conversations. How many times have you heard divisive statements about our genders and sexuality like "Women think with their hearts, men with their genitals" or "Women need to feel loved to want sex; men need to have sex to feel loved"?

While there may be some truth to these statements for *some* men and *some* women, by taking a dichotomous approach to understanding men and women we seem to forget that we exist on a spectrum and don't belong in two separate boxes marked "he" and "she."

I'm certainly not going to suggest there are *no* differences between the sexes—biologically speaking, there most certainly are. And valuable information can come from considering men and women separately and analyzing our sexual differences. As just one example, we have made huge advances in sex therapy and sex education since uncovering that women's sexual desire tends to be responsive in nature (versus the more spontaneous desire men report).[1] Understanding this difference has allowed us to measure women's desire more accurately and treat women's sexual desire concerns more appropriately.

However, in our quest to understand men's and women's sexuality we have developed a problematic habit of highlighting and focusing on *any* differences, regardless of how small, over and above any potential similarities—to the point we are speaking about all men fitting in one box over here and all women fitting in another nice and tidy box over there.

I'll give you an example using one of my favorite sex studies.

237 REASONS

Researchers Dr. Cindy Meston and Dr. David Buss at the University of Texas conducted a fascinating study of reasons that humans have sex. They determined *237* unique reasons![2] Some of those reasons included "I wanted to achieve an orgasm," "The person had a desirable body," "I was bored," and "To get back at my partner for having cheated on me."

After the researchers developed their list of reasons humans engage in sex, they looked to see whether there were any significant differences between men's and women's endorsement of those reasons. In other words, they asked whether men reported engaging in sex for any reason over and above women (and vice versa). Their analysis concluded there were some "significant gender differences."

So what are those differences?

The authors found that men and women were significantly different in their rating of slightly over half of the reasons (123 of the 237 reasons, to be exact). They also found that men were more likely than women to state they had sex for several reasons including physical ("The person had a desirable body"), opportunistic ("The person was available"), physical pleasure ("It feels good"), utilitarian ("To improve my sexual skills"), and social status ("To brag to my friends"), whereas women outranked men on only three items: "I wanted to feel feminine," "I realized I was in love," and "I wanted to express my love."[3]

Seems like the kind of finding that plays right into norms and stereotypes about men and women, doesn't it?

But wait.

The authors also present a list of the most commonly endorsed reasons (of the original 237) for having sex that men and women reported. Here are the top ten endorsed reasons for men and women.

The top ten reasons for men (in order):

1. I was attracted to the person.
2. It feels good.
3. I wanted to experience physical pleasure.
4. It's fun.
5. I wanted to show my affection to the person.
6. I was sexually aroused and wanted the release.
7. I was "horny."
8. I wanted to express my love for the person.
9. I wanted to achieve an orgasm.
10. I wanted to please my partner.

The top ten reasons for women (in order):

1. I was attracted to the person.
2. I wanted to experience physical pleasure.
3. It feels good.
4. I wanted to show my affection to the person.

5. I wanted to express my love for the person.
6. I was sexually aroused and wanted the release.
7. I was "horny."
8. It's fun.
9. I realized I was in love.
10. I was "in the heat of the moment."

Out of 237 reasons men and women engage in sex, 8 of the top 10 reasons (in other words, the most important, relevant reasons) are *identical*. If we were to continue down that list, it turns out that 20 reasons of the top 25 reasons for engaging in sex were *exactly the same* regardless of gender. And there's more! I'm going to get technical here for a minute, so bear with me . . .

The response scale (as with the vast majority of scales in social science) had a range of 1–5. Specifically, the question asked, "I have had sex in the past because . . . ," followed by each of the 237 reasons, and participants were to rank each reason on the scale, with 1 indicating "None of my sexual experiences" and 5 indicating "All of my sexual experiences." As an example, men (on average) endorsed having sex with women "because it's fun" at 3.57 and women (on average) endorsed having sex with men "because it's fun" at 3.05, which was found to be "significantly different"—even though *both* men and women endorsed it as one of their top ten reasons for having sex.

This is what is so tricky with social sciences. Finding something statistically significant is a hugely important measuring tool to determine whether there are differences in our data. And Meston and Buss did a thorough and academically sound analysis to arrive at their conclusions. I'm not trying to pick on their study. In fact, the reason I chose their study to discuss here is because it's so interesting and well done that I think everyone should know about it.

But what I question in many studies that use these types of scales (including some of my own) is the real-world significance. Specifically, is there *really* a meaningful difference in .5 points on a scale of 1–5? Is that enough to conclude confidently that men and women are different? Particularly when they *both* report having sex "because it's fun" in the top 3 percent of their motivating reasons?

Stating that men and women are inherently different in their sexual interest and reasons for sex might be simplifying things a bit too much.

But, as researchers we report the statistical significance (which is crucial), and the media and journalists circulate the findings in a digestible and simplified format (which is the reality), and we are exposed again and again to the same familiar message, rather than the more complex and nuanced version, and conclude men want more sex than women.

MIND THE GAP

I could go into each and every study I have read that seems to have a similar pattern of dichotomizing men's and women's sexuality (for a sex research geek like me, it's tempting!). But instead I'll highlight a larger study that summarizes a great deal of sexuality research on men and women that suggests we might be far more similar sexually than different.

Dr. Janet Hyde, a professor of psychology at the University of Wisconsin–Madison, is a leading expert in the field of sex and gender differences. Her most notable work has been conducting a meta-analysis on gender differences with regard to sexuality over time. (A meta-analysis is a thorough review of all of the research conducted on one topic followed by an analysis to see if there are any trends or larger conclusions that can be made. It's a ton of work and hugely informative.)

Upon completion of her analysis, Dr. Hyde documented that across seven large national data sets between 1993 and 2007, there were very few and very small differences in sexuality between men and women.[4] Specifically, across all of the sexual measures, indicators, and behaviors studied, she found that men reported only "slightly" more sexual experiences (i.e., more sexual partners) and more permissive attitudes than women (i.e., it's *OK* to have multiple partners).

She further noted that most gender differences in sexual attitudes and behaviors were "small" and even smaller in countries with greater gender equality (e.g., Canada and the United States).

The one exception? Men reported engaging in more frequent masturbation.

YEAH, WHAT ABOUT MASTURBATION?

Yes, let's talk about masturbation. Because you might be thinking, wait a second—isn't that a strong indicator that men have a stronger sex drive than women? Because men masturbate more than women do?

Well, yes. Sort of.

I'll concede that some research has concluded that men have a stronger interest in sex than women.[5] But—and it's a *big* but—there are issues with the way sex drive has been measured in past studies, precisely because it's a hard thing to measure.

Think about it—if someone were to ask you how often you experienced sexual desire, how accurate would your response be? Every day? Three times a week? Twice at the beginning of the month but not for the last five days? Does it count when I started to think about sex but then the phone rang and I got distracted? It's not so easy to pin down.

Because of this, researchers have had to come up with certain variables that can be used to tap into sex drive, such as "How often have you masturbated in the last week?" And, when researchers look at men's and women's sexual motivation through reported masturbation frequency, men *do* in fact report more frequent masturbation.[6] And, as a result, we conclude that men have more sexual desire.

But what if masturbation *isn't* the best tool to measure sexual desire?

THE S WORD

Pop Quiz: Do *you* masturbate? Did you masturbate this week? How many times do you masturbate in a month?

If you're a woman and answering these questions makes you even *slightly* uncomfortable, you're certainly not alone. There are pervasive social norms and expectations about what men and women feel they *should* do, particularly when it comes to sex and masturbation. As we discussed in The Origin of Myths chapter, starting at a young age, boys are able to see their penis stiffen and often become more comfortable touching and fondling their genitals. Girls, on the other hand, have their genitals tucked inside and do not get a visual sign for when they might be sexually aroused. Further, young girls are often taught not to touch their vagina because it is at best "unladylike" and, at worst, "dirty." Then over time men are more likely to be praised for having an interest in sex or pursuing sexual partners. Women, in contrast, are more likely to be judged and chastised for the same behavior. Because of these social norms it's pretty difficult to draw meaningful conclusions from self-reported data that use measurements that tap into things men have been groomed to embrace and women have been groomed to ignore or deny.

So, when men are asked about their masturbation tendencies, their answer is more likely to be "How often?" versus a yes or no. Women, on the other hand, tend to be shyer about this topic. Some might blush at the question and ask themselves, "Should I admit that I do?" And then there are those women who actually don't feel comfortable masturbating because they were told they shouldn't. Or because they internalized feelings that it is dirty and they should only get sexual stimulation with, and from, a partner.

That does *not* mean, however, that just because women don't masturbate, or don't *say* that they masturbate, they do not feel desire.

In a very clever study, Michele Alexander from the University of Maine and Terri Fisher from Ohio State University aimed to uncover the degree to which social norms might impact men's and women's reported engagement in sexual behaviors.[7] The researchers were specifically interested in masturbation, number of sexual partners, and watching pornography, to name a few topics. Participants were divided into three different groups who all responded to the same set of questions, albeit with different circumstances.

The first group of participants were led to believe that the research assistants (their college-aged peers) would be able to see their answers once they submitted their surveys. The second group were connected to a lie detector test and told the machine would "know" if they weren't reporting truthfully (it was in fact a bogus test, but the participants did not know this). Finally, the third group were also connected to a lie detector test but only while completing their demographics scale, and then it was taken off for the sexual behaviors survey.

The researchers found that when men and women believed their peers would see their responses, men reported *higher* frequencies of masturbation and women reported *lower* frequencies of masturbation. However, when men and women were told that they were connected to a lie detector test, these gender differences all but vanished. (The group who did not wear the lie detector test and did not believe their answers would be seen scored somewhere between these two groups.)

These findings have *huge* implications for what we think we know based on self-reported sexual behaviors. Specifically, they suggest that both men and women tend to play into the roles we have been given about men having more sexual interest and women having less. But when pushed to give *honest* answers those gender gaps greatly decrease.

Most men masturbate and they do so somewhat frequently. But many women *also* masturbate and may do so more than we typically talk about. Further many women feel desire but do not masturbate as a result. Thus we have reason to seriously question the conclusions from studies that use these types of measures about men's and women's sexual desire as drawing meaningful conclusions about men's and women's true sexual experiences.

DESIRE DISCREPANCIES

Another challenge with trying to make comparisons between men's and women's desire in sex research is that men and women are often studied in isolation. That is, men (or women) typically participate in a research study, but their partner does not. As a result, in the vast majority of cases, researchers cannot verify the participants' perspectives.

So, for example, if a group of men sampled for a study claim to have higher desire than their female partner, we are unable to determine this key piece of information: *would their female partner agree with their claims?* Or, perhaps, would they see things a little bit differently? That's important information, especially if we want to truly compare men's and women's experiences and understand how sexual desire functions within a relationship context.

Only a handful of studies have been conducted on sexual desire in a dyadic relationship (i.e., a study that includes two individuals who are in a relationship with each other). However, the studies that have been conducted arrive at similar conclusions. Particularly, we see that when we explore men and women who are in the same relationship, men are no more (or less) likely to be the partner in the relationship with higher sexual desire.

The first study to document this pattern was conducted almost two decades ago. Researchers from the University of Georgia studied a group of seventy-two undergraduate, heterosexual couples who each reported on their own sexual desire and their perceptions of their partner's level of sexual desire.[8] Although the purpose of the study was to explore the degree to which desire discrepancy (the difference in the amount of desire two partners have) impacted sexual satisfaction and relationship satisfaction, an additional interesting piece of information came out.

Specifically, half of the couples reported no desire discrepancy at all (i.e., the man and the woman in the relationship both indicated they wanted sex about the same amount). Perhaps not what you might expect if you assumed that men's desire is *definitely* higher than women's, is it? Now for the kicker: of those couples who reported desire discrepancy (when one partner had higher desire than the other), men and women were *equally likely* to be the one with lower sexual desire.

This means that half the time women wanted sex as much as men (or should I say, men wanted sex as much as women?), while about one-fourth of women wanted more sex than their male partners and about one-fourth of men wanted more sex than their female partners. So if *only about 25 percent* of the men in this study were determined to want more sex than their female partner, it is hardly appropriate to conclude that men are more interested in sex than women. Right?

But that's not the story we usually hear.

As a social scientist, I know it's never wise to use one study to make a sweeping statement about behaviors. But the University of Georgia study is not the only one that has documented these results!

More recently my colleague and dear friend Dr. Kristen Mark, a professor at the University of Kentucky, and I conducted a similar research study on men's and women's desire in a dyadic context to explore desire discrepancy in romantic relationships.[9]

The sample was, again, a college-aged group of heterosexual men and women who were in relationships with one another. The man reported his level of desire and the woman reported her level of desire so we could compare the results. Again, about half of the heterosexual couples reported the same level of sexual desire (i.e., there was no discrepancy noted). And, similar to the University of Georgia study, in the other half of couples, men and women were equally likely to be the partner with lower desire.

This finding has also been replicated in a study with over 2,300 men and women in the United Kingdom, in which 59 percent of women (i.e., *more* than half of the women) reported that they had higher sexual desire than their male partner. [10] I could go on and on, but you get the idea: study after study continues to suggest that men's and women's sexual desire is more similar than different.

Which brings us to an important question: *why* do so many of us continue to believe that men have higher desire than women when research simply does not support those claims?

MEN CAN'T READ THE SIGNS?

Let's start with why some men tend to believe that they have a higher interest in sex, because many men *do* believe they have a higher interest in sex than their female partners. In fact, when I interviewed men for my research, a lot of the men described that they had a higher interest in sex than their girlfriend or wife. Just take a look at some of these quotes:

> "I've never met a woman who wanted to have sex more often. I think usually it's been the reverse probably."

> "I would want sex way more often than my partner would."

> "I think I've always had the more active libido."

> "I get the impression I feel more desire than [my wife]."

It's possible that these men truly had a greater interest in sex than their partners. As we've discussed, it seems that we reliably know that about one-fourth of men do have more interest in sex than their female partners. However, recent research suggests that men may not always know when their female partner is in the mood, which has huge implications for men's perceptions of their own desire in comparison to their partner's interest in sex. Let me explain.

Dr. Amy Muise, a professor at York University, and her colleagues asked men and women, who were in long-term relationships with one another, about their ability to detect their partner's interest in engaging sexual activity.[11] In other words, they wondered, "Do you know the signs your partner gives when they are feeling horny?"

Over the course of three different studies—that included 44, 84, and 101 (largely heterosexual) couples, respectively—men and women reported on their own daily level of desire and the level of desire they perceived their partner to have. Then the researchers compared these reports to see how accurate men and women were at detecting their partner's interest.

The researchers concluded that while *women* were pretty good at knowing when their male partner was interested in sex, men were found to miss *many* of their female partner's cues of sexual interest across all three studies. As a result, men were led to believe that their female partner had less of an interest in sex than *she* reported having. Or, put another way, women actually have more of an interest in sex than men (specifically their male partners) believe them to have.

This is an interesting concept: women might have *more* sexual desire than we previously thought because (a) we have been overstating small differences between men and women, (b) we have been focusing on faulty measurements of desire (i.e., masturbation) that fall prey to social norms and expectations, and (c) women may actually feel desire at many times but they aren't explicitly showing it and/or their male partners aren't noticing it (more on that when we get to the *initiation myth*!).

WHY THIS MYTH IS A PROBLEM

Believing the myth that men are more interested in sex than women (as with many of the myths I'll address in this book) pigeonholes men and women into certain roles related to their sexuality.

If we believe the myth that men's desire is higher than women's, then when men *do* have lower desire than their female partner, instead of being seen as a *completely* normal variation from couple to couple, it can be perceived as a serious problem that requires fixing. And this can lead to a great deal of stress and worry that is completely unnecessary.

Let's start with the female partner.

When we assume the female in a heterosexual relationship is the partner with lower desire, she is not afforded the same opportunities to embrace and act upon her desires, or to realize the full potential of her sexuality. If she starts to feel her desire is higher than her male partner's, perhaps she begins to quash it, quiet it, tuck it away because it's not very "ladylike" or it's not the way it "should" be.

And, unfortunately, sometimes when I work with couples where the woman has more sexual desire than the man does, I see the woman having the most difficult time. Because she, too, believes that her male partner should have more desire than she does. So she denies her sexuality and possibly adds pressure by criticizing her partner when he isn't in the mood. Sometimes this is because she takes it as a sign that her partner isn't as interested in *her*.

And then there is the man.

You've probably heard men say that they wish they could find a female partner who was super into sex, or that they fantasized about a woman who was enthusiastic about having sex every day. That is, until it happens. Because what they might really be thinking is that it might be fun to be with a woman who has *as much* desire as I do—not more. Because a desire discrepancy (no matter the direction) always leads to some level of tension and difficulty. [12]

In fact, the men I have worked with often describe feeling deeply perturbed as a result of having lower desire than their female partner, worrying it suggests they are not "manly" enough. They often describe feeling concerned, frustrated, and even embarrassed that their desire is not as high as it "should" be. Instead of being excited and sexually aroused by a partner who, in contrast, seems like she is always in the mood for sex, men tend to feel that something is wrong. And more specifically, something is wrong with *them*. I've witnessed men who worry about their ability to perform and satisfy their female partner when she has a higher interest in sex than they do. Essentially, they may find themselves doubting their abilities as a lover.

Men who have a lower interest in sex than their female partner (either always or perhaps suddenly, even temporarily) sometimes even find themselves trying to *prove* they have higher levels of desire than they really do. For example, they may engage in sex or even initiate sex that they are not truly interested in, just to keep up appearances for their partner. And that can create a lack of authenticity and presence during a sexual encounter.

Essentially, when couples believe the myth that men have more desire than women—yet find themselves in a situation in which the reverse is true—they can work themselves into a tizzy trying to make sense of their situation and figure out what's "wrong." And, from my experience, couples can unfortunately come up with *plenty* of relationally damaging reasons.

Women: Consider this an opportunity to reflect on your sexual desire in the context of your relationship and the larger social messages you have received and continue to receive about your sexuality—and then decide if you want to begin breaking down any of those walls.

Specifically, ask yourself whether you might be comparing your sexual interest to that of your partner (is it higher/lower/the same?) and whether you have any expectations about what either of you *should* experience that could be impacting your sexual expressions. Ask yourself, if I could ignore those comparisons and expectations even for a moment, what would *my* interest in sex actually look and feel like? How often do I feel desire? How strongly? When? It can be so freeing to realize that you might have an interest in sex that you've not yet fully noticed or embraced.

Second, if you believe you might be experiencing higher levels of sexual desire than you've been letting on (to yourself or to your partner) consider whether your partner knows. Maybe you feel like you're shouting your interest from the mountaintop and he's missing it. But maybe, just maybe, your signs are a little hard to read. A little on the subtle side. It could be *hugely* fulfilling to embrace your sexual desires more than you have been "trained" to do. Some women find it liberating to step out of their box of "demure" and into "sexual powerhouse." Consider telling your partner an example of when you've been in the mood and ask if he noticed. If he didn't, come up with your own couple language. A sign that you both know means *I'm in the mood.* One couple I worked with put a green sticky note on the fridge when sex was a go that day.

If your male partner is not interested in sex as often as you are, it's *always* worth checking in and making sure things are OK. As we discussed earlier, lower desire can be a result of illness, stress, relationship troubles . . . the list goes on. *But* also try to leave room for his lower interest in sex to be a completely normal male variation. You might want to ask yourself, could I accept my partner as having less desire than me? How does it feel when I'm interested and he's not? Do I internalize that experience as a reflection on me? What would it look or feel like if I did not take his lack of interest as a personal reflection on me or his interest in me?

And if he just doesn't want sex when you do, consider treating him the way you would want to be treated if you were in not in mood. Guilt trips and put-downs are the last thing that is going to get him genuinely interested. But sitting with him and talking about his higher-than-normal stress or just watching a movie together on the same couch might still leave you feeling close and connected.

Men: For those of you feeling your desire *is* higher than your female partner, consider that she may have more sexual desire than you realize, that she *could* want sex at times and you're not noticing or aren't fully picking up on her cues. Just because she might be saying no when *you* want sex, doesn't mean she's not interested at other times. Pay attention (better yet, ask!) and be flexible.

Along those same lines, given what we know about women's desire being just as likely to be higher than men's, there is a chance she is feeling desire but other things are getting in the way. Many women have sexual desires that they don't fully acknowledge or act upon because they are feeling stressed or too bogged down with other life demands to feel like sex is appealing or worth it. Think about it this way: imagine the possibility that your girlfriend or wife has as much desire as you or more, and ask yourself—what could I do to help her unlock it?

On the other hand, if you have *lower* desire than your female partner, it's worth examining your feelings about that and embracing your true sexual interest instead of pretending or feeling pressured to perform at times when you're not interested. Ask yourself, what messages have I received about being a man and my interest in sex? Did I learn that men should want sex all the time? Did I learn to always be interested in sex, particularly if a woman is? What is it like when I'm simply *not* in the mood when my wife is? Could this be OK? Would *she* be OK with it? The sooner you disentangle the two constructs (men = always wanting sex), the healthier and better you will feel and the more authentic connection you will have with your partner when your sexual desires do align.

MYTH IN ACTION: JARROD AND ANNA

The Case of the Elusive Erection

Jarrod was thirty-eight. He was a small-business owner who was charismatic, confident, and a huge baseball fanatic. Anna was thirty-six. She worked as a project manager for a boutique business firm. She was smart and thoughtful and passionate about everything she pursued, from running to photography. Jarrod and Anna had been together for five years. They attended therapy because they were quite distraught about the impact Jarrod's self-diagnosed erectile dysfunction was having on their relationship.

Jarrod had done some thorough groundwork for trying to understand his erectile difficulties. He had met with a doctor to see if there were physical or biological reasons. He met with a naturopath to see if alternative medicine might help. He was trying to eat right and exercising to stay healthy. But nothing was working. So he and Anna decided to come for therapy to see if there might be something psychological going on.

There were two main pieces that came out during our meetings. First, the couple described being on the same page sexually at the beginning of their relationship and described their sex life as fun and satisfying. However, after the honeymoon phase it became clear that Anna had a higher interest in sex than Jarrod.

Anna was vocal about what she wanted from Jarrod in order to experience an orgasm. She was confident and comfortable initiating sex; she wanted to try new positions and experiment in bed. But Jarrod described increasingly feeling that he could not keep up and could not please Anna as often as she wanted. He said he felt a high degree of pressure as soon as Anna was in the mood for sex. He described feeling so worried that he could not perform, that he actually could not perform. A textbook self-fulfilling prophecy.

The second piece was that Anna said she was worried that Jarrod's inability to get and maintain an erection meant that he was not attracted to her. And perhaps he didn't even care for her, or love her, as much as he used to. She doubted herself and looked for more and more reaffirmation through sex, which cycled into more pressure for Jarrod and lower sexual performance. This dynamic was wearing down the relationship in other ways. Self-doubt. Pressure. Insecurities. And this had been going on for months. So the pressure was mounting more and more with every sexual interaction.

Why couldn't Jarrod get an erection? Well, he could and pretty frequently, actually, but just not spontaneously when Anna was suddenly in the mood a few hours after they had sex earlier in the day. Or not late at night after a difficult day at work when he was starting to think about sleep. Essentially his penis functioned just fine. He just didn't have an interest in sex as often as Anna did. And that lower interest made it pretty difficult to get an erection every time Anna wanted it. Ultimately, the pressure that *both* Jarrod and Anna placed on Jarrod to perform decreased his desire to have sex as a way to avoid the disappointment.

Over the course of our work together we had to confront the messages that were holding both back from being able to enjoy sex in their relationship: Could it be OK if the couple accepted their different levels of desire (with Anna having more of an interest in sex than Jarrod) as *normal*? And could the couple find a way for Anna to feel wanted and reassured outside of Jarrod's sexual performances?

Both struggled with these concepts and our progress did not happen quickly. It took us a number of sessions to reconsider how Anna could accept the other ways that Jarrod was expressing his interest and attraction toward her outside of erections when *she* wanted to have sex. Eventually she was able to accept compliments on her physical appearance, "just because" gifts, and gestures to spend quality time together as all part of Jarrod's love, affection, *and* sexual attraction to her. We discussed how it was important to view sexual activity as one of *many* ways that the couple connected. And Anna worked on reducing the pressure she was putting on Jarrod to have sex every time she wanted it. The couple found a way for Anna to embrace her own sexuality outside of their partnered sexual activity, including masturbation and buying a new sex toy.

Jarrod also had to work on reconnecting with his "manly" and confident self, which had taken a bit of a hit due to his misconceptions about his libido being problematic and his erections being elusive. He also had to learn to not let his worry about being unable to please Anna get in the way of the majority of times he was completely able and interested in having sex with her. He had internalized the pressure to perform even when Anna had taken a step back in her sexual demands, and that became the biggest piece of the work. How could he be a "man" and not want sex as much as his girlfriend? Over time the couple accepted and ultimately embraced their sexual pattern. Their new understanding reduced feelings of pressure and actually helped Jarrod get and maintain erections more frequently and easily.

SUMMARY

While there is a pervasive societal belief that men have higher desire than women, sex research is increasingly rejecting this "fact."

- Taking a dichotomous approach to understanding men's and women's sexuality tends to overstate our differences and ignore the variation within each gender.
- The "gender gap" is closing with regard to men's and women's sexuality in many areas.
- Social norms and expectations about the way men and women "should" be impacts men's and women's responses to sexuality questions. When pushed to give *honest* answers, versus socially desirable answers, these differences all but vanish.
- Dyadic analysis (research on two individuals who are dating one another) reveals that men are no more or less likely to be the partner in the relationship with more desire. In other words, in any heterosexual relationship women are just as likely as men to have a higher interest in sex.
- It is possible that some men *believe* they have more of an interest in sex because they are missing some of their female partner's cues that she is "in the mood," and women are downplaying or dampening their sexual interest.
- Accepting it is normal for men to have lower desire and women to have higher desire can reduce judgments and stress about normal heterosexual variation and lead to more satisfying, authentic sexual experiences.

MYTH 3

The Physical Appearances Myth

"**I**t all started when Jordan stopped watching me change into my nighty before bed," Kira muttered as she looked down at her hands. Then, pointing to her midsection, she said, "Now I have . . . *this*. I'm getting older. He just doesn't look at me the same way anymore."

"I tell her she's beautiful all the time!" Jordan retorted.

Despite Jordan's efforts to reassure Kira that he still found her very attractive and that he still desired her, she didn't believe it. She didn't *feel* it. How could she when earlier in their relationship he would "eat her up" with his eyes whenever she walked into the room? Or playfully smack her butt when he walked by her in the kitchen?

Now, two kids later Kira said she could see her body morphing with each passing year. As a stay-at-home mom she had swapped out cute shirts and jeans for any clean shirt she could find and sweatpants. She said she just didn't feel *sexy* anymore. And she could sense Jordan just didn't see her in the same way. He didn't look at her with lust. He didn't initiate sex with the same hunger. She just didn't feel desired by him like she used to before they had kids.

"When we first started dating you couldn't keep your hands *off* me! You used to give me that *wink* and I would know what you were thinking. I miss that wink. . . . There's just no more *passion* in our relationship," Kira said with a mix of longing and frustration. "I'm just your wife now.

A mom. I don't know, maybe we can't get that spark back. Maybe those days are just behind us . . . "

"I still *want* you," Jordan said as Kira looked back down at the floor.

* * *

Perhaps more than any other myth in this book, the myth that men's desire is primarily driven by physical appearances is the one that paints men as particularly surface level. It disregards men's deeper thoughts and feelings, and completely ignores the depth and complexity of his sexuality. And while looks matter to all of us to some degree, after hearing from hundreds of men over the course of my research I can confidently say that men report that their sexual desire is more often, and more deeply, triggered by being with their partner in so much more meaningful emotional, and even *romantic*, ways.

Unfortunately, because our society promotes such a narrow, surface-level stereotype about men's sexual desire, far too many women end up missing the much deeper and much more meaningful ways that their male partner is sexually turned on by them that go *so* far beyond the shape of their bodies or what they are wearing, and many of men's emotional bids for connection go unnoticed.

BUTTERFLY CROWNS AND MAYFAIR FILTERS

I'll admit it. In the world of Instagram filters, enhanced-beauty Snapchats, and one or two photos on dating apps to determine if we swipe right or left, there is no question that looks matter. I am not going to try to argue that they don't. We make decisions about whether we are attracted to someone (or not) within moments of meeting them. This doesn't mean that we *all* find the same people attractive—although arguably there is *some* consensus around the most beautiful people (*hello*, John Krasinski!). But chances are *you* were initially drawn to your partner's physical appearance in some capacity in order to move on to the next stage of dating and developing a relationship. Maybe you liked their charming smile, soulful eyes, or cute butt. Even if someone else would have passed your partner over, *you* noticed.

However, despite the fact that looks matter to all of us to *some* degree, we receive countless social messages that women's sex appeal is *particularly* important to men, while women will overlook good looks for a good personality. For example, there is no shortage of romantic comedies in which a dorky, frumpy (even comically ugly) guy is somehow funny or nice enough to gain the attention of a considerably more conventionally attractive girl. Think Adam Sandler and Drew Barrymore in *The Wedding Singer*, Seth Rogan and Katherine Heigl in *Knocked Up*, or literally any romantic pairing in *Superbad*. And while the message that women are able to see past physical appearances to his personality is arguably a good thing, the second part of that message, the one that says men are always drawn to the most sexually attractive woman—sometimes even blinded by her beauty—does a serious disservice for men and women.

MADE YOU LOOK

The root of our belief that men's desire is primarily triggered by physical characteristics can be explained in part by evolutionary theory. As I mentioned in The Origin of Myths chapter, it has been theorized that men have evolved to notice characteristics of women that would indicate they are healthy and fertile, thereby increasing men's chances of procreation.[1] Larger hip-to-waist ratios; youthful, clear complexions; and so forth. Think Scarlett Johansson, Megan Fox, or Jennifer Lawrence.

And it's true that *some* research supports the proposition that men's desire is triggered by surface-level characteristics. For example, in their famous study "Why Humans Have Sex" (which you may remember from the chapter The Gender Myth), researchers Meston and Buss found that one of the greatest gender differences between men and women is that men were significantly more likely to report engaging in sex because they found the woman's body desirable.[2] In other words, men were more likely than women to indicate they had sex with a partner because of physical appearance alone.

Similarly, men over the course of my research often describe how their sexual desire is triggered by physical characteristics, such as their partner's hips, legs, or breasts. In fact, when I've asked men what sparks their sexual interest, they frequently start by describing their female partner's sexual appearance. For example, Conor described in detail the parts of his girlfriend's body that could turn him on. He said, "I really like the physical shape of her. She has big hips and butt and down to her thighs. And it is the most perfectly drawn line. It defines a large shape but it looks really good." And Terry said it was his wife's legs and calves that when exposed turned him on: "I like it when she cleans . . . when she is working . . . I find it attractive when you can see her leg muscles or her calves. I find it really attractive."

Sometimes it's not even specific body parts and shapes that men describe turning them on; instead they simply indicate that no matter what their partner looks like, her just being naked (or getting naked) triggers his desire. One of the men I interviewed said he responded sexually to his partner whenever she wasn't wearing clothing. When I asked when he tends to feel the most sexual desire, Tyson answered, "Like if she's changing or she's naked," and Travis similarly responded, "I'm excited just if she undoes her bra. Just seeing her I'm excited."

But even these comments, which on the surface appear to support the appearance-driven male desire, are more complex than meets the eye. The first quote from Conor was about his wife, who is considered medically obese. The second participant was describing his wife, a mother of three who was pregnant with their fourth child. And the last two participants, who described being turned on by their partners' naked bodies, were both in their fifties (with wives in the same age bracket). So you can forget any preconceived notions about these comments being the sexualization of young, fit, and perky twenty-year-old women's bodies.

And these aren't just a handful of carefully selected, obscure quotes that go against the grain of what I hear from men *all the time*. Because men have been telling me over and over and *over* how turned on they are by their female partner's body, in all its changing shapes and sizes, and how their attraction, and corresponding sexual desire, goes so much deeper than those conventionally young, curvy, movie-star body types.

So, yes, looks matter. But when we talk about men and sex the conversation seems to come to an abrupt halt right . . . around . . . here. We acknowledge that men are sexually attracted to women's bodies and seeing naked women makes them think about (or want to have) sex. Period. Full stop.

But it's *so* much more than that.

THE C WORD

Countless men over the course of my research have described an ability to pick up on their female partner's level of confidence and explicitly highlight this over and above her physical appearance. They say their desire has nothing (or nearly nothing) to do with her body or what she wears but it's *completely* linked to how confident she comes across. In fact, a lot of men in my research identify when their partner puts on weight or ages but say they still find her sexually desirable because of how she carries herself. Take, for example, Max: "I enjoy her body and confidence more than ever before. She may not look like the model on the cover, but her confidence makes her the sexiest woman." Or men, like Lucas, who downplay the importance of physical appearance in favor of their partner's attitude: "My partner's physical appearance is somewhat important to me. . . . What does turn me on is her attitude."

Confidence matters for a few interconnected reasons, but primarily and most commonly it's because men perceive it as a reflection of women's own feelings about themselves and their attractiveness. Which just so happens to be pretty freaking contagious. As Kyle put it, "For me, confidence in oneself is directly connected with my sexual desire towards them."

Actually, a number of men throughout my research said they didn't care at all about looks; for many it was *just* attitude. For example, here are a few participants describing the importance of confidence: "When she is confident in herself it is very sexy"; "I have always valued comfort and confidence as part of sexual attractiveness, and that has not changed. I don't really care what she wears as long as she is happy with it"; and finally, "What matters most is how she feels about herself and her willingness to share herself with me."

I could go on.

But while men describe being physically drawn to their female partner when *she* feels good about herself, when her confidence is *lower* chances are it decreases his level of desire, too. Damon described how after his wife gave birth he could see that she gained weight, but he said that didn't matter to him; he still found her attractive and very desirable. However, her own negative perception of her body diminished his sexual interest. He said,

"She was always physically attractive. And recently, [since] our kid that we have together, her weight has always been a bit of an issue. And it's played a little role in the way her and I would be physically, I guess. So when I don't see that confidence, because she does have confidence even though she's concerned about her weight. Now she's losing confidence and she acts like she's losing confidence. And that's, I think, a little bit why I don't think about her a lot sexually."

Many, many men I've spoken with have echoed the notion that they care less about a woman's appearance and more about her attitude. As another example, Daniel describes that it is not his wife's physical appearance that affects his desire, but how *she* feels about her body. He stated,

"I'm a bit of a health nut. And I don't feel nearly as much sexual desire if my partner is not confident. They don't have to be in amazing shape. But I want them to at least feel confident and do good things for themselves and their body. And for me, it's sometimes hard to have that sexual desire if that's not there."

He went on to describe his experience of feeling turned off if he felt his wife was trying to hide parts of her body during sex. He expressed that he wanted to feel she was fully present and vulnerable during sexual activity, and if he noticed she started covering up parts of her body, his desire would diminish. He said,

"Sex is something that's extremely intimate and it's, you know, you want it to be, you want each other to completely give each other. . . . So I find if you're not confident, they're always holding back. Or, you know, I don't want in the middle of sex to hear "I want to leave my shirt on." If you want to leave your shirt on because you want to leave your shirt on, that's fine. But if it's because you're very self-conscious and you're not self-confident in yourself, I don't respect that. If that's the case, that's one thing. But if you're not doing something about it and complaining about it . . . then that to me is my number one killer of desire."

I can say this with a great deal of (*ahem*) confidence and certainty: I've *never* met a man in my professional career who has talked about not being sexually turned on by his female partner. Not once. They may *prefer* when she wears something sexy more than when she wears sweatpants, and hygiene and cleanliness are *definitely* factors. But far more often it is the female partner who feels that *she* has let herself go, no longer feels sexy or on top of her game, and *she* pulls away first. Not him.

I WANT TO HOLD YOUR HAND

I can still remember a conversation I had early on in my research that confronted my own biases about men and sex. I was speaking with a man in his late fifties named Greg. He was a calm, mellow, nature-loving, bird-watching hippie. He talked so beautifully and lovingly about the relationship he had with his wife and how much he absolutely adored her. When I asked about how he experienced sexual desire, he responded that sometimes the two of them would sneak off in the middle of the day for a glass of wine. Or go for long walks to look at and listen to the birds. Or close the office early so they could spend hours upon hours talking.

As much as I thought these descriptions were sweet as all get out, I started to wonder if we were digressing from the topic of sexual desire. Did he mean that he just *enjoyed* doing those things with her? That they led to feelings of *love* and *closeness* and *connection*? Not *desire* though, right?

But he was very clear about this: these activities *were* sexual desire for him. It's not just that they spurred on desire (although they did that, too). He said that he felt desire for his wife *during* all of these activities, whether or not they had sex after.

It was only after hearing from more and more men in my research and in therapy that I started to realize that men *were* talking about desire when they described these moments. These men were telling me—right to my face—that they felt desire just holding their wives' hands. It didn't mean it led to sex. But it was a slow-building, low-simmering kind of desire that made them feel truly connected and more likely to want to have sex at a later time. For example, Marcus said,

> "My desire is there simply by being around her. It is her that I'm attracted to, and that attraction rises to the surface when I'm near her (or think of her), not because of any particular choice she has made regarding her appearance."

As another example, Christopher described how his sexual desire *used* to be a purely sexual thing earlier on when he and his wife were first dating. But now he acknowledged, later on in his relationship, that while other people might view certain activities as nonsexual, for him they were sexually charged. When describing his experience of sexual desire he said,

> "Some people would view it as nonsexual . . . like cooking her break-fast and taking it to her and maybe, yeah, sitting there and holding her hand. Or even laying there by her feet and watching TV."

And while I've heard from various men about different, sometimes even unexpected, ways that their desire is experienced well outside the con-fines of the bedroom, there are three bigger examples that seem to be more generalizable to men across my research.

COME TALK TO ME

> "Sexual desire from the men's side is twofold. The first is visual. And two is mental or intelligence. The intelligence of the person and how you connect and talk and laugh together and communicate."

I love this quote because it so clearly articulates what countless men have shared with me. It's from a conversation I had with Tony, where he was highlighting a critical piece about men's sexual desire that so many of us fail to recognize. Visual cues are important to men, as we know. But the second side, the *deeper* side of men's desire, is triggered by the kind of things that can only happen when there is a deep connection between two people. Feeling connected, laughing, and having meaningful conversa-tions. He isn't describing love. *This* is desire.

Men also frequently tell me that engaging in communication with their female partner leads to a deeper connection and understanding of one another. And it isn't "only" an emotional connection. Many men describe how this increased level of intimacy could often lead to their interest in sexual activity. As Alex described, "We haven't talked in a while. So let's put the kids to bed and let's just climb into bed and let's just talk. But it's not uncommon for connecting with talking, you know, that we become intimate physically with each other."

For some men, intimate communication sparked closeness and could sometimes be the catalyst for sexual desire. Jeremy described the circumstances in which he was having an intimate conversation with his long-term girlfriend about something that had previously caused tension in the relationship. When they talked about it and saw things more from the same page, he said it made him feel more emotionally connected to his partner and led to a more memorable experience of sexual desire, primarily because he felt seen and understood by his partner:

> "We were having a conversation. I'm a musician and we were having a conversation about my music. Because my band is on hiatus right now, which is a stress to me. Or it's, I feel a sense of loss. But she also, we were talking a lot about my music and we were getting in deep into what I play, and how I play, and what she thinks I should do with myself as far as music goes. . . . Her being so interested in something that has caused some friction in our relationship, like validating it."

Communication is frequently included in lists of ways to improve a couple's sexual satisfaction.[3] But as the quotes I've shared with you highlight, it's not as simple as just conversing. Talking about whose turn it is to take out the recycling or making a financial budget for the next month is not so likely to produce that same sexual interest.

The key piece here is feeling *heard*. Being on the same page. Feeling connected, close. And while feeling that connection is a well-documented sexual enhancer for women,[4] "we" (that is women, men, and our society in general) don't tend to acknowledge that feeling emotionally close is a critical piece in men's experience of sexual desire.

NIGHT TIME IS THE RIGHT TIME FOR ROMANCE

Cuddling on the couch and watching *The Notebook* may sound more like her preferred date night in than his. But I'll say it throughout this book until my face turns blue: men are more touchy-feely than we have been giving them credit for. Based on my conversations, in therapy and in research, there is no shortage of men who have mentioned that they are more likely to be interested in having sex during, or following, a romantic date night that is some variation of what I just described.

For example, when I asked what circumstances might be at play when men feel more sexual desire, one of my participants responded: "I'd be more sexually interested if we went to the movies, out for dinner, a pleasant evening." And another said one his most positive experiences of sexual desire would include

> "a nice candlelit dinner, maybe a bottle of wine . . . maybe watch like she says a girly movie or something, a 'chick flick' and yeah, cuddling on the couch, both getting into that feeling, groove, vibe. And then from there, taking it into the bedroom."

In fact, when asked what an "ideal" sexual desire experience would look like, one participant responded, "It would be like, you're out for a nice dinner, you know, she's dressed nice. That sort of thing. You just have a nice evening in that way. That's my ideal. We kind of go on a date."

These men aren't describing what they think their *wife* wants to hear. I collect these responses from them privately—without their partner around. She would never hear or know these answers unless he chose to share them with her. This is what *he* wants to do. What *his* ideal sexual encounter looks like. It's a far cry from the stereotype about men being ready for sex at the drop of the hat—*anytime, anywhere*. Or that romance is only important to women, and men begrudgingly go along with cheesy date nights because they have to.

Can (some) men have sex at the drop of the hat without any build up or romantic context? Sure. But that's the story we *always* hear. The tired, one-note mentality about men's sexuality pulsating out of their bodies and how they are ready to go any time. I'm suggesting that *sometimes* men might just be interested in the softer side of sexual desire, one that aligns a little more with what we might think of as being stereotypically important to women. Going on a nice romantic date can be a slow-burning sexual tension build up for him. It's not necessarily about what's to come after—because let's be real, in long-term relationships, sex doesn't always follow a date night out like it may have when we were first dating. The feelings men get by having a romantic date night with their partner just might *be* sexual desire.

SO FAR AWAY FROM ME

So far we've talked about communication and romantic settings as being factors that facilitate men's sexual interest. And the thing that ties these two pieces together is that they both facilitate the experiences of closeness and intimate, emotional connection. Which, again, is so much more important than appearances. As Aiden says, "Her looks play a role, but we are connected on a deeper level so it is emotional also."

In fact, emotional closeness is so important to men's experience of sexual desire that if you're *not* feeling emotionally close, chances are his desire won't be there. Fraiser explained,

> "If our emotional connection is under a bit of strain and we're disagreeing about something that can't be solved quickly because we're working it out. My desire to have sex with her will go down. I want to feel like we're on the same page. And sometimes that can't be resolved terribly quickly."

To drive this point home, Fraiser described how the sexual frequency between him and his wife was on the lower end—once a month or less. So when she initiated and he felt they hadn't worked through an issue, it could be another month before they had sex again. And he still said no. Think about that in contrast to that crazy idea that all men want sex *all* the time!

In response to a question about circumstances within his relationship that were detrimental to his experience of desire, Warren shared that arguments and misunderstandings with his partner would decrease his desire: "I guess with a lot of frustration, or I guess misunderstandings, or when we're not connecting at all." Further, while many men I speak with say they don't like to turn down sex when their wife offers it (although they do, of course, and we'll get to that in The Opportunity Myth chapter), Chase expressed that he would say no if he felt he and his wife were not on the same page or connected: "Me saying no has only happened a couple of times, just because of my frustration and anger towards her at the time."

What I'm saying is that most men I've spoken with are unable to separate their sexual desire for their partner from their emotional connection. Romantic setting and meaningful conversations help give men that feeling of closeness that is a real turn-on for them. On the other hand, if you're *not* getting along or spending quality time together, chances are men are not going to be so interested in sex.

WHY THIS MYTH IS A PROBLEM

The myth that men are primarily motivated by physical appearance is particularly limiting to men's sexuality, which has negative consequences for men *and* for women. There is nothing wrong with being turned on by good looks, lacy lingerie, or revealing clothing. Most of us are, to some degree, and there is nothing wrong with embracing it. However, the belief that men are primarily (or worse, *only*) turned on by women's physical appearance shortchanges couples from experiencing a number of other bids for sexual and, perhaps more importantly, intimate connection.

Women: Women's sexual desire is *hugely* impacted by how desirable we feel.[5] We know from the research that women report feeling more turned on, sexy, and sexual when they feel wanted by their male partner.[6] Accordingly, when we have a limited belief about what turns our partner on, we unfortunately miss the more complex, nuanced, and meaningful ways that he feels desire for us.

So while physical appearances count to a degree, so much matters to men's sexual interest over and above your appearance, like meaningful communication, romance, and emotional connection. If you're missing that spark or doubting his sexual interest, consider whether you might be missing some of the *other* less stereotypical (and, as a result, less obvious) ways he is showing his desire for you. Just because it may feel more subdued than those earlier "I want to rip your clothes off" days doesn't mean his desire for you isn't still there. And consider that men report that close connection, feeling on the same page, and meaningful conversations with the woman they love are *key* facilitators of their desire over and above physical appearance.

I don't know if there is a woman alive who doesn't want to know that their husband or boyfriend isn't feeling more desire by feeling romantically drawn to her than she might have previously thought. It's just about challenging some of our assumptions and inviting that desire in.

Men: Don't worry—I'm not suggesting your wife stop wearing sexy lingerie! In fact most men I talk to say they love when their partner gets dressed up in something sexy. But most often it's because it's fun and different or it's sexy to see her feeling confident or carefree.

I've never met a woman who doesn't appreciate being told she looks beautiful and sexy by the man she is in a relationship with. So whenever you think it, *say it*. It's ultimately on her to believe, feel, and embrace, but no harm comes from reminding her about what *you* see when she walks into the room, especially if she seems to be a little down on herself.

Second, and more importantly, she may not notice your sexual desire in ways that we are less socially trained to see or expect from men. So if you feel desire for your partner when you're feeling close and deeply connected or when you're sitting on the couch having a meaningful and stimulating conversation, try to find a more explicit way to share this with her. Perhaps lean over and give her a kiss on the cheek. Or tell her how sexy you find it when you're debating current political events and she one-ups you with her insights into foreign trade. Or when you're having a blast listening to records and debating which is your favorite Beatle (the answer is George Harrison, by the way). You get the idea. Whatever it is that turns you on outside of her looks, *share that*. Feeling desired is a huge aphrodisiac for women (and for men, too, as we'll discuss in great detail when we get to the chapter The Desirability Myth) and the more she feels *your* desire for her, the more desire she just might feel in return.

Finally, from time to time, bask in the warm, sweet glow of that low-burning desire that can show up during the types of romantic, emotionally meaningful moments I described earlier. Just because you feel desire when you're holding hands doesn't mean sex has to (or even *should*) follow. This could just build up the passion and excitement for better, more passionate sex at another point down the road.

MYTH IN ACTION: KIRA AND JORDAN

The Case of How Kira Got Her Groove Back

Kira longed for the passion she and Jordan experienced early on in their relationship when they first started dating. She described feeling disconnected from her younger, sexier, pre-motherhood days. And she felt like Jordan's desire for her just wasn't as strong as it used to be.

Except that, as you now likely know, Jordan *did* still find Kira sexually attractive. He tried telling her this but Kira had a hard time hearing it. "You're just saying it because you have to," she would say in return.

Jordan indicated he just wished that Kira would see what he saw. That he wanted her still. But, Jordan admitted he had noticed Kira pulling back and he wasn't sure how to respond: "I used to feel like you *wanted* me to watch you change," he finally said one session. "Now, you're racing to get from your clothes into your pajamas. You don't even face me— you're hunched over like you don't *want* me to look." He said he felt a bit detached and distant from her. Like she was in her own world, thinking about the house, the kids . . . definitely not him. So he stopped looking as much at her before bed and started focusing on his book instead.

We started by focusing on Kira's sexual self-esteem. It was important for her to feel good about herself, no matter where the rest of our couple work took us. I asked her to think about when she felt good, more confident, and even a little bit sexier, what she was doing at those times and why it helped. Kira decided that something as small as wearing jeans and a shirt instead of sweats at the end of the day made a small but meaningful difference. She felt more like "Kira" and less like "just" a mom. Spending an extra moment or two naked after she got out of the shower felt bold and confident and awoke a little piece of her that had laid a bit dormant since having her kids. It reminded her of the single Kira that used to walk around naked in her apartment alone while she cleaned. Why did she need to hide? She looked *good*. And, more importantly, she *felt* good.

I also asked Jordan to describe to Kira what *he* found attractive and desirable about her. It's always nice to hear what our partner thinks about us, and Kira was having a hard time letting in Jordan's compliments so far. The "you're so beautiful" sentiments weren't sticking. I asked him try something else. He didn't miss a beat:

> "I was just thinking how turned on I was by her last night when we were at a dinner party with our friends. Kira was so charming and funny. So 'on' and in her element. She seemed relaxed and like she was having fun. It reminded me of when we first started dating. And she sat beside me and put her hand on my leg while she was telling a story. It felt so good. I could have kissed her right then. It felt like we were 'Kira and Jordan' again."

Over time Kira slowly but surely began to notice—and accept—the other ways that Jordan was turned on by her, not just because of how she looked, but he was turned on by her intellect. Their conversations and laughter over romantic dinners. When they played chess and he looked at her while she thought deeply about her next move. He was turned on by holding her hand on the couch when they watched a movie after the kids were asleep. It wasn't just looks of *love* in these moments. Sometimes they were looks of desire. But just to make sure these feelings weren't being missed, I encouraged Jordan to share his desire at these times in a way that would help Kira notice them. The couple came up with a little love language of their own. Instead of just making eye contact, when Jordan felt that desire grow he would give her that trademark wink Kira so missed.

SUMMARY

Women's sexual desire is hugely impacted by how desirable they feel to their male partners. Consequently, the myth that men are primarily driven by women's physical appearance is not only limiting to men; it is damaging for women's sexual self-image and discounts men's other bids for sexual intimacy.

- According to evolutionary theory, men are thought to be motivated by physical characteristics, which would help them find, and mate with, potentially fertile women.
- Sex research has typically focused on these surface-level aspects of men's sexual desire and attraction, which reinforces these stereotypical beliefs.
- While looks and appearances matter, men describe valuing a woman's confidence and comfort with herself over and above any physical attributes.
- Further, there are deeper and more meaningful reasons that men feel desire that go way beyond physical appearance, including romantic situations, intimate communication, and emotional intimacy.
- Limiting men's sexual desire to being mainly triggered by physical characteristics reinforces a narrow stereotype about men and sex

and often results in women's inability to accept and let in the deeper ways their male partner is feeling and demonstrating his desire.

MYTH 4

The Selfish Myth

"**W**e missed our window *again* this month," Ella said, clearly annoyed. "I told Aaron that we needed to have sex three times this week, and *definitely* on Wednesday. But he worked late and made some lame excuse each time. And now we missed our chance and have to wait until *next* month!"

Ella and Aaron had an eighteen-month-old son and were trying to conceive a second baby. Well, at least it was clear that Ella wanted another child. I was still trying to get a sense of Aaron's wishes on the matter. So, during our individual session, I asked Aaron about his thoughts on potentially growing their family and becoming a father of two.

To my slight surprise, Aaron said he *was* really excited about the idea of having another kid. He shared that he came from a family of five and always wanted a big family of his own. Which left me feeling somewhat perplexed. After all, he was avoiding sex during Ella's more fertile days, and I couldn't help but infer that he had some reservations about having more children.

Then Aaron explained: "We've *barely* had sex since our son was born. I know it takes time to heal, but it's been a year and a half and we have *maybe* had sex four or five times. And now Ella wants to get pregnant again and suddenly she wants to have sex all the time and thinks I should be happy about it. But she doesn't want to have sex with *me*, she just wants to have sex to have a baby. There is no passion or romance. She just tells me 'it's time' and lays there passively like it's a business transaction." Then Aaron said the words I have heard from more than a handful of men in this situation: "I just feel used."

* * *

Throughout this chapter we will tackle the myth that men are *so* sex crazed that they will happily take whatever sex they can get. In other words: the myth that for men, having *any* sex is better than having no sex at all. The reason this myth is *oh* so wrong is because it implies men are not concerned about the *quality* of the sex they are having, and more specifically, it implies that they could enjoy themselves just fine during sex *even* when their female partner isn't that into it. And, when put like that, what woman could possibly get herself in the mood for *that* kind of sex?! Yuck.

But this myth couldn't be *further* from the truth. What we know from the research is that women's pleasure and sexual enjoyment is actually one of the *biggest* motivators for men during sex. And most men would rather not have sex at all than have it with a female partner who they feel is distracted, not really "into it," or just passively waiting for it to be over. That's because most men want to have sex to feel connected and close, not to just "get off."

THE BAR IS OFFICIALLY ON THE FLOOR

Tell me if you've heard this one before: Two guy friends are talking. One is in a relationship and one is single. They're doing some version of the grass-is-greener-on-the-other-side-of-the-fence thing. The guy in the relationship makes an offhand remark about how nice it would be to live the bachelor life—watching the game uninterrupted in his gitch, and not having to worry about cleaning the house for his in-laws who are coming over for brunch first thing in the morning. And then the *single* guy who has been striking out left, right, and center in the dating world says, "Yeah, but at least you're getting laid."

The message underlying this statement isn't "You're so lucky that you're having sex with someone you love!" And it's not "It's cool that you get to be held and hugged and touched." And it's certainly not "That's awesome you're having mind-blowing, passionate, orgasm-filled sex!" In fact, it's not even about *quantity* of sex. It's just a comment that reveals an assumption that on *some* level, the guy in the relationship is having *some* kind of sexual activity. However good, however often, at least it's sex! And that should be better than nothing at all. At least it sounds pretty good to the guy *not* getting laid.

But, as many of us in longer-term relationships know all too well, the act of having sex isn't always *that* satisfying. Sometimes *not* having sex at all feels like a better option than having dissatisfying sexual encounters with a partner we can just tell isn't that into it.

In other words, when it comes to sex, no man wants to feel like his female partner is just throwing him a bone (pun fully intended).

WORLD'S WORST HAND JOB

Have you ever seen the show *Breaking Bad*? I'm kidding, of course you have (and seriously, if you haven't, put this book down right now, binge watch it, and come back later). While there is no shortage of incredible scenes in this show, the one that will *forever* stand out in my mind is where Skyler and Walter are lying in bed and she gives him the *worst* hand job of all time.

The scene starts with Skyler sitting in bed with her laptop. She's in the middle of online shopping and she reaches under the cover and starts giving Walter a hand job. No build up or anything. She just grabs him. He says, "What's going on here?" somewhat suggestively. She says, "You tell me, *birthday boy*" equally suggestively. But *then* she keeps looking forward at her computer, and while she continues to rub him dispassionately, they start having the most mundane conversation imaginable about the car wash and a road trip to a museum. Walter *yawns*! The scene ends with Skyler shouting in excitement that her purchase went through, while Walter seemingly struggles to maintain his erection and we are left to assume the sexual activity stops right there.

This scene so accurately depicts a very unfortunate, yet prevalent, mentality that shows up in far too many sexual encounters between men and women and ultimately results in really, *really* bad sex. The belief is that men are *just* looking for physical gratification. That he just wants to get off. His sexual needs are surface level and physical. The sexual activity doesn't even have to be very good. As long as his penis is rubbed long enough that he comes, he's getting what he wants.

And for a woman, what could be a *worse* headspace from which to enter into a sexual relationship with her male partner? She certainly wouldn't feel cared about. She certainly would not feel seen. And she would probably feel like her pleasure is secondary or perhaps not even a consideration! It sounds like a really bad one-night stand. Not the kind of sex we want to have with the person we love.

THE MOST IMPORTANT THING

The good news is men want so, *so* much more than one-sided physical gratification when it comes to having sex. That is, men want to *connect* with their female partner and to feel that she is present with him and enjoying the sexual experience as much as he is, and perhaps even more so.

So just how important is a woman's sexual pleasure to men during sex? Over the course of my research, men have told me almost without fail that their female partner's sexual pleasure was *paramount* to his sexual experience and his own sexual pleasure. And, in some cases, they have told me that her pleasure is even *more* important than their own. Here are just a few examples:

> "It's very important to me that my wife experience sexual pleasure and I get just as much enjoyment from her pleasure as I do from my own."

> "This is my primary concern when having sex."

> "This is the cornerstone of sexual intimacy."

> "Number one concern every time. My pleasure is secondary to her being pleased."

> "This is essential. Like most men, her pleasure is an innate part of my enjoyment."

That last quote "like most men" is particularly poignant. This participant isn't describing his own unique brand of preferences around giving sexual pleasure. Rather, he is sharing that what *he* experiences is what he feels *all* men want. And, given how often women's pleasure is described as being of utmost importance to men in my research and during therapy, I must say I'm quite inclined to agree with his insights.

In fact, when describing the importance of giving their female partner sexual pleasure, a number of men in my study said that if they only cared about *their* pleasure they would sooner masturbate. For example,

> "If I minded about my pleasure I'd go alone."

> "It is of utter importance. I can always find satisfaction. My goal is to satisfy her."

> "If I just wanted to have an orgasm there are other ways to go about it. Sex is an art—an acquired skill. When two people have sex it should be about the other person. . . . Bottom line, if she's not enjoying it there is no need to do it."

Men in my research also described that watching women experience pleasure (and particularly pleasure that they are in some way, shape, or form responsible for providing) is a *huge* turn-on for them. But don't just take it from me. Here are a few of the men in my research explaining what they personally get from seeing their female partner experience sexual pleasure:

> "There is nothing more arousing than her breath/voice and the way her hips roll when she is getting off. Participating in that experience is so much more sexually satisfying than my own orgasm."

> "Her joy is my joy and it makes me feel awesome to see her in ecstasy. She has a stressful life and I love seeing her let it all go."

> "Pleasing her greatly increases my desire. And it's a huge win for me because focusing on her pleasure extends our sexual experiences."

(Hang on to this, because when we get to The Desirability Myth chapter, I'll expand on how women's sexual enjoyment actually makes men feel *desired*, which as we will come to see is a huge component, perhaps even the *biggest* component, of men's sexual desire.)

PERFORMANCE ENHANCER

But back to the importance of women's sexual pleasure to men's sexual experiences. It should be clear now that women's sexual pleasure is hugely important to men during sex. But it raises an important question: why does *women's* sexual pleasure matter so much to *men*?

You may remember from The Origin of Myths chapter that there are some pretty big and powerful social messages that men and women learn when it comes to sex. And for men that includes things like pushing to the next level of sexual intimacy, doing the desiring and not being desirable, *and* being sexually experienced and skilled in order to provide pleasure to their female partner.[1]

In that sense it's not *just* that men like their partner to experience pleasure as a purely altruistic gesture (if there even is such a thing), and it's not *just* because men get turned on by watching women experience sexual pleasure. It's that on top of all that, men often experience some validation or reward, if you will, that he is doing his "job" of *providing* pleasure. That is, men describe that their female partner experiencing pleasure is essentially a barometer of his sexual skill. For example, Eric said, "[Seeing my girlfriend's sexual pleasure] makes me feel great to genuinely believe I'm a good lover." And Fernando echoed, "It's a measure of my ability to satisfy her needs."

In other words, part of why women's sexual pleasure matters so much to men is because it falls under that traditionally masculine expectation for men when it comes to sex. That is, men are *expected* to be sexually skilled,[2] which means providing pleasure or bringing her to orgasm. So, if men *don't* see (or feel or get a sense) that their partner is experiencing pleasure—or more specifically, if they feel that they aren't satisfying her sexually—they can experience a real blow to the ego. As Lochlan described, "There is the ego thing . . . if she's not enjoying having sex with me, either I'm doing it wrong or I'm not paying enough attention to her emotional/mental state, which makes me feel I'm failing my partner."

Yes, you read that right. He said "failing." Like it's a high school report card. Pass = orgasm, fail = no orgasm. If you're starting to get a sense of how this dynamic may have some pitfalls and damaging effects, well hang tight, because we're just getting started.

HER ORGASM, HIS ACHIEVEMENT

Researchers Sara Chadwick and Dr. Sari van Anders, at the University of Michigan, recently conducted a study that explored the interaction between over eight hundred men's self-evaluations related to whether their female partner had an orgasm.[3] The men were randomly assigned to read one of two scenarios. In the first scenario men were asked to imagine that they were engaging in sexual activity with an attractive female partner. He could tell she was enjoying herself, she made passionate noises and got louder and louder until—fireworks!—she had an orgasm. Sounds pretty good, right?

Then there was scenario two: Men were again asked to imagine they were having sex with an attractive female partner. However, this time he was told that she wasn't that turned on or sexually excited. Then as *he* reached his climax, she—well, nothing else happened for her. She didn't have an orgasm. End scene.

Then the researchers asked men questions that tapped into two constructs: sexual self-esteem (how good or bad you feel about your sexual skills) and *masculinity*.

Chadwick and van Anders found that when men read a scenario in which they imagined their female partner having an orgasm, they felt better in terms of their sexual self-esteem *and* they reported feeling more masculine. In contrast, those who read the second scenario in which they imagined that their partner did not orgasm reported lower levels of sexual self-esteem and reported feeling *less* masculine.[4]

This finding is nuanced. On the positive side, it reinforces the point that men are *highly* motivated for their female partner to experience sexual pleasure during sexual activity.

The *not-so-good* news is that when there is such a high focus and narrow attention on having (or giving) an orgasm, (1) we can lose sight of all the other elements of pleasure that can be experienced during sexual activity (touching, caressing, kissing, holding each other close, etc.), and (2) it puts *a lot* of pressure on men during sexual activity because, well, what happens when women *don't* have an orgasm?

IF YOU'RE NOT INTO IT, NEITHER AM I

Sex without an orgasm—or, at least without *some* kind of physical peak, climax, or sexual excitement—isn't *necessarily* bad sex. In some cases it might still feel nice. Like a really intimate hug. Other times it's just . . . *meh* . Lackluster.

And when women are not experiencing a whole lot of pleasure during sex they can get inside their own heads. Maybe they're trying to figure out if there is a way to get into a better position for more clitoral stimulation. Or they're focusing their attention on their breath in an attempt to relax or tap into the sexual experience more authentically. Or women might even find that they've mentally checked out of the sexual situation and their mind is wandering to that really awkward interaction with the new boss. . . . And in these situations, women might wonder if their husband is picking up on those nonverbal signs on some level. If he notices that they're losing interest. That they're not moaning with great enthusiasm. That it's just not doing it for them right now.

Well, I can tell you this. Men most certainly *do* notice when women aren't enjoying themselves during sex. In fact, when I asked men how they knew their female partner wasn't into sex, they described picking up on *countless* signs and indictors. Cues ranged from lack of communication, nonverbal body signs like tightness and clenching, and their partner looking distracted. Here are a few examples:

> "Yes. Lack of feedback and interest. It was very demoralizing."

> "Her body wasn't reacting, I could feel her mind was elsewhere, her eyes were closed and body tense. No matter what I did she did not seem to loosen or relax."

> "She wanted no foreplay and just immediately wanted to go to intercourse. During intercourse, she would make faces and noises as if she was experiencing some pain. I'd ask her if she was feeling pain and she'd say 'no,' and that she was fine."

> "She may seem distracted or even start talking about nonsexual things."

Because their female partners' sexual pleasure is paramount to men, when they pick up on the signs that their female partners *aren't* enjoying themselves all that much, they take it personally and shut down emotionally.

That is, in stark contrast to finding women's experience of sexual pleasure intoxicating, men have told me over and over again that if their female partner is not experiencing pleasure (say, if she is distracted or just not that into it) it's a *huge* turnoff. Here are just a few examples:

"If my partner is not experiencing pleasure then neither am I."

"It would be a huge turnoff if she didn't experience sexual pleasure."

"If my partner is not enjoying herself or is in any way burdened by the time we share, it is a massive turnoff."

"I feel like she's just placating me if we have sex and she gets no enjoyment from it."

Hopefully it's pretty clear that women's sexual pleasure is of utmost importance to men's sexual experiences. So what happens when women feel that their sexual pleasure doesn't matter to their partners, and when men notice that their female partners are not experiencing sexual pleasure?

CAN YOU JUST HURRY UP AND FINISH ALREADY?

"Are you done yet?" Whether women say these words exactly (or some variation) or give some of the nonverbal cues described earlier, it just doesn't feel good to get the impression that your partner was ready to stop having sex thirty seconds ago, if possible. As Elliot described, there is a feeling he gets from his wife when she is ready for sex to end, something that feels pretty unpleasant and unsettling. He said, "The 'let's get this over with' energy is yucky and 'I'm doing this for you instead of with you' energy is gross."

In order to get out of that unpleasant feeling, I often hear from men that their strategy is to just hurry things along. As Cory described, once he can tell his partner isn't into it, he just wants the feeling to end so he tries to come as fast as possible: "My response can vary, from politely trying to hurry and finish, to losing my erection/desire outright." And while this strategy seems to be a frequent go-to move, most men say that it feels pretty awful and something they would sooner avoid altogether. Fernando described, "The act feels rushed when she's not into it. It makes me feel like a chore, almost worse than outright rejection."

If you're following along, here is a quick summary of the sex men and women are having far too often, guided by our belief in the *selfish myth*:

1. Women are consenting to have sex that they aren't really that excited about but think they are doing their male partner a solid, because "obviously" he just wants to get off and seriously any sex should be good enough for him, right?
2. He can tell she's not into it, which takes a blow to his ego and possibly his masculinity. He realizes he's not getting what he really wants from sex (connection, closeness, her pleasure) so he starts rushing sex to get it over with but isn't enjoying the process.
3. She feels him rushing, which only reinforces that he's mainly focused on getting off.

So when it's all laid out on the line like this (is there a loudspeaker around here?), *why are we having sex in these situations*?!

Well I'm going to suggest that maybe you shouldn't. Because as I said from the outset of this chapter, men are saying they would rather not have sex at all than with someone who is just waiting for it to be over. And if said female partner is just waiting for that sexual encounter to be over anyway, well you get where this is going.

NO SEX IS BETTER THAN BAD SEX

I just really want to hit this point home. Despite the myth that for men *any* sex is better than no sex at all, men in my research consistently state that they would rather not have sex at all than have sex with a partner who is not into it. As Jerry said, "I would generally rather not have sex if one of us is really not in the mood." And George went into a little more detail about how his wife was continuing to consent to sex that she didn't want and that it felt so awful he ended up putting a stop to it:

> "There was a window of time in which she offered and pressed for maintenance sex. She understands sex as an important part of marriage

and really wanted to provide that even though (likely due to medications) she wasn't really into it. These experiences were awful. . . . I stopped accepting because a dead bedroom is better than this alternative."

The feelings men experience when they are having sex with their wife and she isn't enjoying herself, range from sadness to resentment to feeling angry and hurt. Ivan described,

"These encounters would make me feel unfulfilled, slightly angry, and hurt. I don't understand why . . . if she truly couldn't get into that mind-set, why she would try to placate me when she should know I'd be able to sense her disinterest."

And Logan added, "She faked orgasm once during masturbation. Since I know her involuntary reactions (stomach muscles, arching back, flushed face) I called her out. I was disgusted. Could have just said no or I don't feel like it."

Stopping in the middle of less than satisfying sex is an OK and even healthy choice to make. Unfortunately women can feel so trained to hide their own feelings (sexual and otherwise) that they make the compromise and have sex because they think *he* wants to continue and they are trying to be "nice" and accommodating. But this belief is not only unfortunate, it's misguided. As Harold described,

"If I ask if she really wants to, or what's going on, she just tells me everything is fine and just do it and that she wants it. For me? I hate it. I've told her fifty times that her body is not a thing I want to use to get myself off. The sense of obligation that she brings into it sometimes makes things difficult, especially as I've also told her many times that I'm not interested in 'obligation sex'—either she wants to be with me out of desire or she doesn't, but feeling obligated to be with me is not sexy or good."

WHY THIS MYTH IS A PROBLEM

Over the course of a long-term relationship there are always going to be less-than-satisfying, I'm-not-*that*-into-this-sex sex. Because sex is no different than any other aspect of our relationships, which have ups and downs, excitement and monotony. We can have amazingly creative, in-spired-by-binge-watching-*Iron Chef* dinners, and lazy, let's-just-heat-up-this-old-leftover-lasagna dinners. We can have deep, meaningful, thought-expanding conversations and "Have you noticed the weather has been kind of cold these days?" conversations. So there are, of course, going to be times when we have sex where one person (or even both people) aren't as into it and aren't getting as much sexual pleasure from it as we otherwise would. But *why* sex is feeling less than satisfying and what we choose to do about it, especially when it becomes a pattern, matters.

Women: There are a plethora of reasons that you might not experi-ence pleasure during sexual activity. It could be a physical one, such as not getting enough clitoral stimulation.[5] Or complicated interactions, and perhaps even misunderstandings, about your personal turn-ons and turn-offs.[6] Or perhaps you find it challenging to be present during sex and fully experience the sexual sensations.[7] Or, really any number of other medical, relational, or cultural reasons.[8] Bottom line: if you're not enjoy-ing sex or are not getting pleasure from sexual activity on a regular basis, it's worth exploring why this might be the case (and you can start by checking out the bibliography at the end of this book).

But there is another possible explanation that many of us tend to overlook: as women, we can set ourselves up for low to no sexual pleas-ure by functioning under the belief that what *he* cares most about during sex is *his* sexual gratification. First, it just feels flat-out gross to think that our partner is only in it for his own needs and not ours. There is no part of a relationship in which it feels good to think of our partner as acting *that* selfishly.

Second, this myth, unfortunately, causes us to miss out on how much our sexual enjoyment matters to our male partner and how hard he is working in hopes of providing us with sexual pleasure. We certainly don't want to *fake* enjoyment or orgasms to make him feel better—that's not advisable *at all*. But if we can invite a slightly different mind-set to accept how much he ultimately cares about *our* sexual pleasure, maybe, just *maybe*, we might feel a little more in tune with, and connected to, him—and that just might mean we are able to enjoy ourselves more during sex.

And third, and perhaps most importantly, if we actually believe the lowest common denominator about men and sex—that as long as *he's* satisfied that's all that matters—we shortchange our own sexual agency by tuning out and not being a fully present participant. We consent to having sex that's more for him than it is for us. Sex that we feel we don't need to be that involved in. And it just follows naturally that when coming from that headspace, the chance of having a sexually satisfying encounter is pretty unlikely. If instead we have sex knowing that our pleasure is of critical importance to him, then we start to be able to shift into a place where we can focus on *taking* pleasure instead of just passively giving it.

Men: Think about how often you are noticing your partner's lack of sexual enjoyment during sex. If it's here and there it's probably nothing to panic about. As with any other part of your relationship, it's OK once and a while to have an off day. Expecting each sexual encounter to be mind-blowing and passionate and exciting is unrealistic and sets yourself up for failure.

But if you're feeling that your partner is not into sex on a regular basis, you are highly encouraged to do some more digging. Is there a reason she might be less interested in sex these days? For example, is she stressed? Upset? Are there emotional rifts in your relationship? Is there something going on at work or with the kids that is leaving her feeling overwhelmed? She has to do her own personal research too, but no harm ever came from a partner being involved in asking these questions as well and considering whether you (or your relationship dynamics) might be playing a role, however big or small.

It's also worth remembering that giving pleasure is not solely your job. You may take pride in your oral sex skills or knowing how to touch her to get her in the mood and that's totally awesome. But she has to learn how to *take* pleasure. If she is hemming and hawing and not giving you any direction or feedback when you ask for it (because you're *asking* for feedback, right?) then she needs to do a little work to better understand what she wants, how to ask for it, and how to share that information with you.

But what I recommend *you* do is to ask yourself whether there is any reason she might *feel* you don't care about her sexual pleasure based on actions you're taking or a vibe you're giving off. Despite the research presented earlier about men often preferring to have no sex over bad sex, it's not at all uncommon to do the other option: rush sex. Which probably just makes her feel like you only care about getting off and aren't noticing the distracted look she's getting in her eyes. If she seems like she's not getting pleasure from sex (*even* if she tells you it's OK to keep going), it's better to pause and try again another time when you're both more into it.

MYTH IN ACTION: ELLA AND AARON

The Case of the Fertility Window

Back to Ella and Aaron and Aaron's ambivalence about trying to have another child. On the one hand he said he wanted another baby (even a few more!). But at the same time Aaron was avoiding having sex with Ella each month around the time that would increase their chances of conception. So let's back up a few months to what led to this situation.

Aaron described how there was a lull in sexual activity after their son was born (which, by the way, is *completely* normal). So when Ella was ready to have more frequent sex in hopes of having another child, Aaron said he was initially pretty excited. But they didn't get pregnant that first month. Or the next month. Or the month after that. The fun started to wear thin and they began holding off on having sex when they *actually* wanted it so that they could save their energy for the "right" days. Sex stopped being spontaneous and started to feel like a chore. A perfunctory tool to get his sperm to Ella's eggs. And although Ella was highly motivated to conceive, Aaron felt she was not approaching sex with any romance, passion, or enthusiasm. It was just down to business.

We highlighted how Aaron was essentially putting up a protest. He wanted a kid, too, but he also wanted to have sex to feel close to Ella—to experience pleasure himself and, more importantly, to provide Ella with sexual pleasure. And every time Ella would lay there passively, looking off at the wall, he felt more and more distant from her. More and more shut down. And then, well, he stopped wanting to have sex altogether and started making up excuses about why he had to stay late at the office.

We started by validating Aaron's experiences about how it made sense that he didn't want to have sex with a partner who wasn't into it and to whom he didn't feel connected. And that it was important for him to voice that feeling close and providing pleasure were crucial for his own sexual interest. We also had to give Ella some space to air her grievances. After all, she was feeling hurt, too. These last few months were also hard on her. She was feeling rejected and frustrated. Like they weren't on the same team. She was paying such close attention to her cycle, telling him it was important that he come home on time, and then he would call again to say he was working late. But at least now she had some answers (and felt relieved that Aaron was on the same page as her for having more kids).

We came to an agreement that the couple needed to carve out time to have close, connected sex with one another again, with no baby-making agenda. We planned that they would try to have sex once a month outside of the "fertility window" and that they would both try to be present and engaged. The focus wasn't necessarily on having an orgasm, but it was about taking some pleasure from being fully in the moment with one another. We also planned that when they were trying to conceive that they would do something that would help Ella feel more in the mood first so it wasn't so procedural (like a date night out, putting on nicer outfits, having a candle lit at the dinner table). They certainly weren't going to be doing this three days a week during her fertile period, but they agreed to pick one day and make it special so that they could focus on themselves in addition to planning for their forthcoming second child.

SUMMARY

The myth that men are just happy having sex and will take any sex they can get (perhaps even with a smile on their face) paints men as incredibly simplistic when it comes to their sexual desire, and it does a great disservice to women's sexual pleasure and enjoyment.

- Men reliably report that their primary motivating factor when having sex is providing sexual pleasure to their female partner. In contrast, if she's not experiencing pleasure, chances are neither is he.
- Men are pretty good at reading the signs when women are not experiencing pleasure during sex. There is no benefit for women to try to conceal or fake sexual enjoyment (and it is certainly not advisable for your sexual or relationship satisfaction that you attempt to do so).

- When men know that women have lost interest or are not experiencing sexual pleasure, their strategy is often to hurry up and come as fast as possible.
- However, having rushed, dispassionate sex is not satisfying for men or women. Lose, lose.
- Men report that they would rather not have sex at all than have sex with a partner who is not feeling it. Sometimes the best move is for him to masturbate or not have sex at all than to have bad, lackluster sex.
- Accepting men's desire to *give* pleasure may help women feel more connected and in tune with their male partner during sex as well as shift from being passive during sex to an active role of learning how to take and accept pleasure.

MYTH 5

The Pornography Myth

"Am I not enough for you?" Alexis asked, sounding somewhat hurt. The question was directed at her partner, Jeremy, who was sitting beside her silently, looking down at his shoes.

Jeremy seemed embarrassed. Or was it ashamed? I couldn't tell yet. But he was certainly more reserved than he had been in our first few sessions.

The context leading up to this moment: Alexis had recently walked in on Jeremy watching porn.

Now, the porn *itself* wasn't necessarily the problem. Alexis didn't have any moral objections to it. She said that she knew most guys watched porn sometimes. And when I asked about porn use in the couple's relationship Alexis answered, "We've never really talked about it. I know Jeremy probably watched porn *before* we started dating. And I'm assuming he watches it when I'm out of town. But this time was different."

"How so?" I ask.

The night of "the incident" the couple was relaxing on the couch watching a movie. After it ended, Alexis went to bed to read a book and Jeremy stayed up to watch some sports highlights. A little while later Alexis was thirsty, got up to get a glass of water, and, much to her surprise, found Jeremy on the couch masturbating to a video on his phone.

"It's not a big deal. It's just porn." Jeremy said, still looking at his shoes.

"But I was home. Upstairs. In bed! You could have told me you wanted to have sex that night. I might have been interested," Alexis said.

"You say that now," Jeremy responded, finally looking up. "But you haven't wanted to have sex for weeks."

* * *

Pornography is a multibillion-dollar-per-year industry with thousands of new videos being uploaded each day.[1] The popular site Pornhub reported that in 2016 they had twenty-three billion visits (that's sixty-four million a day!), and in the same year 4.599 billion hours of porn were watched on their site alone.[2] And whether you've watched porn yourself or have just seen some of the click bait, it's pretty obvious that the *primary* target audience is heterosexual men. So the question isn't so much *whether* men watch porn (because most do, or at least have); it's *how* men interact with porn, the relevance and importance it has in their sex life, and, of course, how that impacts their intimate relationships.

Unfortunately, the default assumption about men is that their sexual desire is so high and insatiable that porn plays a critical role in their sexual interest *and* their sexual repertoire. That there is something about porn that satisfies men in a way that can't be experienced in their romantic relationships. But in this chapter I will challenge those assumptions and suggest that men's relationship with porn is the exact *opposite* of this myth. I'll demonstrate how men's sexual desire is primarily *relational* in nature, and as a result porn most often plays a minor and peripheral role in men's sex lives. I'll also highlight that men almost *always* prefer having partnered sex, because it's *connection*, and not just physical gratification, that men truly crave.

THE X-RATED FILES

I don't think there is a woman alive who hasn't wondered to *some* degree about her male partner's pornography use.

Is he watching porn?
What kind of porn is he watching?
How often is he watching? For how long?

When does he watch it?

Did I almost just catch him that time I surprised him when he was on
   his computer?

Does he watch it when I'm at home? When I'm asleep?

Does he want to try that stuff with me?

Does he want to try that stuff with her? With them?

And quite frankly, it's *good* to be curious about your partner's porn use.
In fact, it's always good to be curious about our partners' sexual behaviors, preferences, interests, and fantasies. And porn, whether a minute
sliver or a more generous serving, is a slice of that sexual pie.

Yet the reason men's porn use remains a mystery to so many women
is largely because it is a private endeavor. Most of us watch pornography
in the privacy of our own homes. When no one else is home. Or at least in
a private room, with the door locked. And most of us don't tend to talk
about our porn use openly.

In stark contrast, women know a lot of other things our male partners
like. We know their favorite sports teams. We know their preferred
brands of beer. We know their most listened-to driving songs. We know
their go-to, I-look-good-in-this T-shirts. All this because we know what
they watch, drink, listen to, and wear. And while there are certainly
couples who talk openly and honestly about their interest in porn, the vast
majority do not talk about their porn use or interests.

PRIMETIME PORN

The positive news is that we *are* starting to see a shift in terms of how we
talk about porn at a social level. I'll give you two examples from two very
different television shows that very recently caught my attention.

The first was on (as you may now know) my favorite show *This Is Us*.
Cut to Kate walking into the bedroom to find her partner, Toby, in his
bathrobe, on the bed, looking intently at his laptop. He quickly shuts the
screen and acts sheepish. But Kate laughs, assumes he is watching porn,
and grabs his laptop to see at what he's looking at. It turns out to be a dog
adoption website (turn on the waterworks!) and the tone of the conversation changes. However, it's a great example of what a reaction to finding
your partner watching porn *could* be. Kate didn't treat it like a threat or
something embarrassing or awkward. Not something to freak out about.

Instead it was something a little funny and, more importantly, interesting to know. *What are you watching? What do you like? What are you into?*

The second was a bit more serendipitous. I was channel surfing one night, going back and forth between some baking showdown and a home makeover reveal, when something juicier caught my eye. A man and woman are sitting in bed and the woman is trying to start a dialogue about porn use. The male character denies ever watching porn (which cued the laugh track, as he was *clearly* caught in a lie). But then the interesting part. *She* tells him that she watches porn and that it's OK if he does too. And that she thinks it would be helpful to talk about what they like to watch so they can know each other a bit better. He acts surprised because—well, she's a woman who likes watching porn, gasp!—but the conversation eventually shifts into a fairly mature interaction about sexual preferences and porn watching habits that brings the couple closer together (note: after a little digging I later found out this was *The Carmichael Show*).

Both of these shows were primetime slots—not HBO at midnight—so the conversations were relatively PG and more suggestive than overt. But that is also what made the scenes so great. They were *just* conversations about porn. Nothing salacious. Nothing shocking. Just an open, albeit a bit awkward, conversation. *What do you like? Why? When do you watch? What parts are you interested in doing? What parts are just fantasy?*

I'll go on record as saying I don't think there is much that is healthier for your sexual and intimate relationship than having these curiosities about your partner. So if you're open to starting the dialogue, I'll start by sharing what I've heard from men about their use of porn and then we'll shift into how important this is for men's sex lives.

MY FIRST LESSON LEARNED ABOUT MEN AND PORN

During my first set of interviews with men, I asked pretty open-ended questions about what helped men feel more or less desire, and intentionally left as much room as possible for *anything* to be shared. And here's the thing: very, *very* few men brought up their interest in, or use of, pornography unprompted. I had to ask nearly every time.

Then, when I asked *directly* about pornography use (i.e., "I couldn't help but notice we haven't talked about porn so far. Does that play a role in your sexual desire at all?"), most men indicated they watched it some-times, but said it wasn't that important to their desire. For example, Robert said that while he looked at pornography once in a while, he felt confused, or at least uncertain, about what his attraction to it was: "If she is maybe at work, maybe sometimes [I watch] once in a month or two months? But it's not desire . . . I have no idea. But I will watch some-times." Another participant similarly described that although there was something sexually appealing about pornography, he did not in any way consider desire to be part of the experience; as he described,

> "As far as like, seeing pornographic images or movies or whatever, typically for me it would be seeing other people engaging in sex, which can be arousing. But it's not really those people. There is a distinction there. . . . There is nothing particular about . . . there are attractive bodies and things like that. But there is a step to desiring them sexually."

Then there were several men who just said things like "It doesn't interest me that much" or "Sure I've watched here and there, but it's not a big thing for me." So, after conducting several interviews I felt justified in concluding that porn just wasn't all that important to men's desire.

But when I met with my advisors, some questions were raised about whether this *lack* of a finding might be a limitation of my study. After all, my advisors are prominent sex researchers and professors of human sexu-ality and they are *highly* aware of the pornography consumption statistics I rattled off at the start of this chapter.

We wondered, was it possible that because I was a woman, men didn't feel *comfortable* talking about pornography use with me? Maybe they were worried I would judge them? Maybe they thought it wasn't polite to discuss in "mixed company"? Maybe if I were a man they would have expanded and talked about how much they loved porn and how much they *really* watched it? All good questions that had us racking our brains.

I'm going to pause our conversation there and come back to it in a moment. Stay with me here.

FINDING A NON-FINDING

Imagine that some researchers are conducting a study on how to improve orgasm frequency in a group of women. They run a three-week course that teaches women about their anatomy, techniques for self-stimulation, and mental relaxation exercises. Then, after three weeks the researchers look to see if the women report higher frequencies of orgasm. Only, they find out the program didn't work. The women report the same number of orgasms before the study and after. No change.

So now what?

In addition to this being frustrating for the women who were hoping for a sexual improvement, the researchers are also stuck with a problem. They don't have anything to report. Journals don't want to publish the findings of trials that *didn't* help women orgasm. Media outlets don't want to hold interviews with the researchers to learn more about their program that *didn't* work. There just *isn't* a finding.

This is what we call the null results bias. It happens all the time in research. We ask a question or conduct a study or develop a program *thinking* we are going to see something change. And those are the results that get published, talked about, and shared. Anything else, well, it gets tucked away or stored in some drawer, never to be seen or talked about again.

Except that, what if *not* finding something is really a finding in and of itself?

Well, fade back to the conversation of me sitting with my committee members talking about my non-finding on men and porn. After a bit of deliberating, my one male committee member spoke up and said, "What if pornography just isn't that important to men's desire?"

We paused and let this sink in. Could it be that my participants *did* tell me everything about the importance of porn? That perhaps we were just assuming porn *must* be important because it is so omnipresent and consumed at warp speeds and that it *must* be important to men's desire? Was this another assumption we held about men and sex? What if men *were* watching porn but maybe just weren't *that* into it?

To me this seemed more likely. After all men had been talking to me about a lot of things that weren't necessarily free from judgment (i.e., I heard about affairs, erectile dysfunctions, and it's not as though any of the men *denied* watching porn). So I jumped back into the research to see if there was other research that might support the possibility that men *watched* porn but maybe it was something that was unnecessarily receiving too much attention in terms of it being a critical piece of their sexual repertoire and interests.

HE'S JUST NOT THAT INTO YOUPORN

Well, it turns out, this non-finding *had* come up before. At the Kinsey Institute in Indianapolis, Indiana (founded by the one and only sex research pioneer Dr. Alfred C. Kinsey), professor Dr. Erik Janssen and his colleagues conducted six focus groups with thirty men about their sexual arousal.[3] This study was different from mine in a key area: this study included groups of male participants with *male* researchers. So you would think that if porn *were* important to men it would come up in that context. Except, even in that situation, somewhere you might think that men could even play into stereotypes or want to appear manly—the researchers *still* reported that the men mentioned a wide and very balanced variety of responses. One participant would say, "I'm a fan," and then a few other men would jump in and say things like "I'm not big on it" or "I think it degrades the real thing."[4]

So while it seemed more and more likely that porn wasn't all *that* important to men's sexual desire, I still wanted to know more about what function it served in men's relationships when they *did* watch it. This time, in order to avoid *any* potential impact my gender could be having on the interviews, I conducted an online study, one in which the participants' identity would be anonymous and confidential. They would know I was a female researcher but I would never know who *they* were, their name, where they lived, nothing. While again I can share that many men said porn was not *that* big of a part of their sex lives, I was able to learn more about the reasons men watch porn.

PORN AS A SUPPLEMENT

So first things first. Perhaps not too surprisingly, one of the most common reasons men report watching porn is because they are in the mood to have sex when their female partner isn't, so they look at porn as something to masturbate to. As a backup, if you will.

If you recall from the chapter The Gender Myth, I shared that men are *equally* likely to be the partner in a relationship with higher (or lower) desire. But regardless of the direction, desire discrepancies happen all the time. In fact they happen in every relationship to some degree. Because there are always going to be times when one person wants sex and the other doesn't. So when one person has a higher interest in sex, whether that be over the course of a long time or just here and there, watching porn and masturbating can be a really helpful way for couples to navigate those sexual differences. As Rowan shared, "I have a way higher sex drive than my fiancée and I balance that out by masturbating (sometimes with and sometimes without porn)."

Tristan gave another example of how he uses masturbation to supplement his higher interest, and how he views it as a helpful activity in his relationship:

> "I've actually found that masturbating has actually helped our relationship. Me personally. That way I don't need to pressure my wife to give me that sexual relief. Then I can just keep her comfortable and take care of her. That's how I've kind of tried to remedy that . . . versus always asking."

Plenty of other men have also described using pornography from time to time to help with masturbation when there were particularly long sexual dry spells in the relationship. For example, "I get off to porn sometimes when my partner isn't interested in sex," or "When we go days at a time without sex sometimes, and porn gives me something to masturbate to."

All in all porn is described by the vast majority of men as simply a way to help stimulate themselves during masturbation between sexual experiences. Not something they sought out or looked forward to doing. Plan B. They wanted to have sex, the opportunity didn't happen, so they search for a video to masturbate to instead of their own memories or imagination.

FEELING LAZY OR TIRED

Dinnertime in our home isn't easy. I'm a vegetarian. My husband is essentially a carnivore. We have a toddler who one day loves pasta and the next day won't touch it, and an infant who only has two teeth and needs bite-sized soft foods. Needless to say, it's a lot of work to find a meal that satisfies us all. And while I love eating dinner as a family, occasionally I feel such relief on nights when my husband has to work late or when our kids are with their grandparents for a sleepover. In the former situation I get lazy and make a Kraft dinner or pizza, in the latter we can make a nicer "grownup" meal. It's a little easier because there is just one (or two) less human(s) to worry about. And then there are the most glorious evenings, when *everyone* is out and I get to eat *whatever* I want. I only have to worry about my needs. These are the nights where I indulge. I'll order in sushi or pad thai from my favorite restaurant and pour myself a large glass of sauvignon blanc.

What do my eating indulgences have to do with porn? Well, when we have sex we tend to spend a lot of time thinking about the other person's wants and wishes. And two people trying so intimately to read the other person is part of what makes sex so special and intimate. But sometimes, just *sometimes*, maybe we don't want to compromise on what sexual position we try. Say our partner wants to spoon, and we want them to be on top. Or we're in the mood for slow sex, and they want it quick and dirty. Or we want to have sex in bed, and they want it on the couch. Or you just want to get off, and they want to hug and take it slow . . . you get the idea.

What I'm saying is that sometimes it's easier to just masturbate on our own to porn than deal with all of that. And when men in my research talk about their use of porn, the most frequent reason they use it is in situations like this. They are tired. They are feeling lazy. They are horny, but they just don't have the energy to seduce their partner. They don't feel up for navigating different sexual interests. And so, instead, they just take a break from all that. They have an itch that needs to be scratched, and porn and masturbation is going to do the trick.

As a couple of examples, some participants in my research said, "Sometimes I prefer masturbation over sex because it's generally a simpler act, since I don't have to accommodate a partner. The pornography just facilitates that."

Or as Joel more crudely, but perhaps just as honestly, put it,

> "Sometimes when you're tired or hungry or your blood sugar is low in my case, you'd like to come without doing any work for it. And it's a selfish thing . . . more a function, merely physical release and getting off."

IT'S LESS STRESSFUL THAN HAVING SEX

I think we can all relate to the experience of feeling too lazy to seduce our partner with foreplay, or to get on top, or negotiate the time, location, or position. But sometimes there is an added piece that plays into the feel of exhaustion: trying to please one's partner sexually comes with a degree of pressure. For example, Tim shared that sometimes he'll watch porn instead of having sex with his girlfriend because he doesn't have the energy to satisfy her. And as we now know from The Selfish Myth chapter, women's satisfaction is hugely important to men's desire. If a man worries that he can't satisfy or please his partner, he may be less likely to reach out and initiate sex and more likely to turn to porn. As Tim shared, "Sometimes I prefer to watch pornography because I am not required to fulfill the needs of another person, and the pressure that creates is relieved." Sean similarly described how porn can be less stressful and that he actually feels nervous having sex or initiating sex with his wife sometimes. Porn, in contrast, is stress- and worry-free so as a result is more appealing to him at times.

> "Often I prefer to watch pornography and masturbate because it can be less stressful/work than having sex with my female partner. When my partner and I have not had sex for a while (a couple weeks to about a month, usually due to physical issues on her part), sometimes I get nervous about us having sex. I sometimes watch pornography and masturbate because there is no risk of having a failed sexual encounter and there won't be any emotional fallout."

Sean's comment also taps into another big myth about men and sex: his reactions to sexual rejection. But that's such a big piece of men's sexuality that I've dedicated an entire chapter to it (we'll get to that in The Rejection Myth).

The thing is, sex functions within the context of our relationships, so it is impacted by so many dynamics that are outside of the bedroom. Power dynamics, disagreements, unresolved fights, insecurities, and the like. So sometimes men describe feeling that sex is the battleground in which other problems play out. And sometimes they want to avoid it. They feel pressure to perform, and they are worried they aren't going to satisfy their partner. But again, the underlying dynamic here is that men are focused on the relationship *first*. However, a rift or disagreement or worry about not being able to please leaves them feeling emotionally shut down, so porn serves as a functional backup option.

PORN IS SECONDARY

Here is the thing I want to really hit home. Almost without fail, *even* when men watch porn, *even* when they like porn, and *even* when they choose to watch porn because they are lazy or worried about their female partner's response, men almost always, *always* say that given the choice they would prefer to have sex with their wife or girlfriend.

I hear this message from men so often and so frequently I feel it needs repeating. So here are an assortment of quotes from several men I've heard from reiterating this fact:

> "Sex is always better. It's more emotional and it feels better."

> "I would always prefer sex with my partner. Porn is a weak substitute for actual presence with her."

> "There's the real world, and the imagination. I prefer real."

> "Sex is way more fun."

> "I crave and value the experience with another person."

> "[Porn] does not come even close to partnered sex."

> "Looking at images on a screen is a very poor substitute for a real partner."

And perhaps my favorite response, which uses an analogy I think we can all relate to, "Why would I want to watch pornography when I could be making love to my wife? That's like the difference between watching someone else's home movie of their vacation or going on vacation yourself."

The reason men prefer their partner to porn any day is because no matter how fun or hot or steamy or sexy a porn video is, men's sexual desire is hugely linked to their emotional connection. Carson described how he didn't really like porn because it did not include the element of a sexual experience that was most crucial to his desire: an emotional connection. As a result he said he didn't enjoy watching porn:

> "Pornography really hasn't interested me. I actually find it kind of gross. Since it isn't relational. I've had the two amalgamate, or I've had the two come together so tightly now that I can't experience anything sexual without intimacy also being there. So if I see two people having sex, I'm like oh well, OK? I'm almost an objective observer of it. Like it's a mammal or whatever. I'm not going to lie, there is some stimulation but not enough I would go seek it out. Unless it is someone I love or an expressed love it doesn't really interest me."

As I've said before and will continue to say throughout this book, men are not so sex crazed that they just want to get off all the time. Men want to have sex because they want to feel close and connected. So while porn and masturbation provides men with a physical release (which arguably feels good), it is not able to satisfy their urge to connect with a person they love. Hugo describes, "I indulge, particularly when there's a period of time when she's not interested in sex for a while (or during her period). It's a release, but it's not like it's fulfilling the way sex with my wife is."

In fact, even if the physical side of desire was taken care of with porn, the real urge to have sex with a partner tends to linger even after masturbation has occurred. As Donald put it,

> "The fulfillment that comes when you're with another person is deeper than it is when you're just by yourself. If you're by yourself you might get that physical release, but it doesn't satisfy the overall urge. So even if you met your own physical needs daily, or two or three times a week, or whatever, it doesn't take care of the longer-term one building up because there is not someone else involved."

The feeling of being disappointed by porn is only intensified when men are masturbating more than they want to (i.e., in situations where they are in sexless or near sexless marriages). Tristan described how masturbating to porn could fill an immediate need but ended up making him feel worse overall:

> "I will use erotica and masturbation. I can only do it for so long and then I have to take a break because I think it's the idea of wanting to be touched, wanting to touch skin . . . it's satisfying for a few seconds and then it's like eating chocolate cake when you're depressed. It feels good while you're eating it but then you feel crappy at the end, because it's not the chocolate cake you really want."

WHY THIS MYTH IS A PROBLEM

Study after study has concluded that it is our perceptions of, comfort levels with, and understanding of porn that impacts our sexual and relationship satisfaction, and not simply whether porn is being viewed.[5] In other words, watching porn is not the problem; it's our evaluations of whether watching porn is good or bad. Every couple has to figure out where and how (or if) porn is going to fit into their relationship. There is no right or wrong way for this to happen as long as both parties are in agreement. But in order to make the best decision we need to have some answers that are based on facts. Not fears, doubts, and insecurities based on the myths about men's relationship with pornography.

Women: Porn doesn't have to be the elephant in the room. Couples benefit greatly from talking openly and honestly about their thoughts on porn, what they watch, what they like, and whether they will use it for fodder for their intimate lives. And the thing is, chances are he is watching as a peripheral *supplement* to your sex life. Because he was really tired one night or feeling lazy after a long, hard day at the office. Or just for something a little fun and different when you're not in the mood or you're not home. The thing I can almost guarantee is that he would prefer to have sex with you over watch porn any darn day of the week. Because my research tells me that men's desire is largely relational in nature. He wants to touch you, feel you, and connect with you. And while porn can be stimulating and enjoyable in some circumstances, you'd be hard-pressed to find many men who *prefer* porn over the opportunity to connect with their wife or girlfriend.

Every couple has to figure out *together* how and where porn use falls into their relationship. Is it a casual supplement? A way to balance out mismatched libidos? Or is it getting in the way of your intimate relationship? If it's the latter and you have more questions about porn than this chapter can offer, I would recommend *The Myth of Sex Addiction* by Dr. David Ley for a comprehensive and well-presented overview of the topic.[6] But by asking these questions, particularly if you're concerned about higher or problematic porn consumption, you may start an important conversation about your relationship, such as his fear of not providing you with sexual pleasure, feeling emotionally detached, or even worries about sexual rejection (if that's a concern he raises, we will delve *much* deeper into that topic later in The Rejection Myth chapter, so hang tight).

Men: It never hurts to consider how and why you're using porn. While porn isn't inherently negative—in fact, it very much can be a positive—if your partner isn't on board it's going to be a sneaky and secretive thing. If she is feeling a bit uncomfortable with it and asks questions, try to be receptive and answer them. It probably isn't easy for her to ask. And your answers are important. An awkward conversation that helps you be on the same page is better than no conversation at all.

If you find your pattern is that you watch porn because you feel lazy or are too tired, it's worth digging a little deeper. *How* often are you feeling too tired for sex? Are you feeling tired because it's been a long day at the office? Or are you feeling emotionally drained from interactions with your spouse? Do you need to focus your energies on getting a better sleep or reducing your workload in order to benefit your relational and sexual intimacy? If you're using porn as a way to escape or avoid a negative interaction with your partner, it's much better to talk through those issues head on.

Additionally, there are other chapters in this book to help address some of the reasons you might be turning to porn more often than you want. If you're worried about rejection, skip ahead to The Rejection Myth. If you're struggling with having a higher interest in sex, maybe check out The Gender Myth. And if your porn use is in the healthy category and your wife isn't worried about it, then, well you're doing great and can give yourself a pat on the back and keep doing what you're doing.

MYTH IN ACTION: ALEXIS AND JEREMY

The Case of the Late-Night Show

Porn wasn't *the* reason that Alexis and Jeremy had come to therapy. But it was part of a recent pattern of events that had left the couple feeling emotionally distant. The passion had subsided, and Jeremy said that these days they "felt more like roommates than lovers."

Jeremy said he had always watched porn here and there. He never felt like it was compulsive or unhealthy. It was just part of what he considered a "normal" sex life. He watched porn before he started dating Alexis, watched less when they got together, and only looked here and there if the mood struck—if he was bored or horny or because Alexis wasn't home.

But over these past few months Jeremy admitted he had been turning to porn more often. He said that when he suggested or initiated sex it didn't seem to go anywhere. He would get the feeling that Alexis wasn't interested. And so instead of putting himself out there and being turned down, he would sometimes watch porn instead. He didn't really want to but at least it scratched his itch.

After Alexis walked in on Jeremy watching porn, they couldn't avoid the topic any longer. Instead of porn being a secretive pastime, Alexis and Jeremy started to talk about it. Alexis said she didn't always realize that Jeremy was trying to initiate sex or that he felt she wasn't interested. In fact, she said she felt *he* was closed off recently and so she had backed off, assuming sex was off the table. It wasn't the *ideal* entry point into this much-needed conversation, but at least they were talking instead of avoiding and ignoring.

Alexis listened to Jeremy's answers about how porn fit and that it wasn't a substitute or a threat to their relationship. And that in fact he deeply missed *their* sexual interactions. The couple came to the agreement that they were both comfortable with Jeremy watching porn as an occasional outlet (and Alexis watched too, by the way). But they agreed that if they were both home, he would put himself out there and check with Alexis first to see if maybe sex was on the table. It wasn't always (and never has to be), but at least the couple agreed that they had let their intimate connection fall to the wayside and it needed tending to. They agreed on biweekly date nights so they could spend more time together and feel more on the same page. They put effort into flirting and talking more. They just found more ways to put each other first. The arrangement wasn't perfect, but relationships never are. However, the couple was able to learn a little bit more about the other's sexuality and they were able to start making the steps to reconnect intimately so that porn wasn't Jeremy's go-to move.

SUMMARY

Men's relationship with pornography is not necessarily as critical to their sexuality or their sexual repertoire as we are so often led to believe. In contrast, because men's sexual desire is largely relational in nature, porn most often functions as a supplement to men's much-preferred sexual activity—partnered, relational sex that provides feelings of closeness and connection.

- The majority of men are not inherently obsessed with porn. Men have a variety of reactions toward watching porn, ranging from enthusiastic to just not that into it to finding porn to be a turnoff.
- When men *do* watch pornography it is often for healthy reasons, including embracing their individual sexuality or helping bridge the gap between sexual encounters when they have higher desire.
- The most common reason men choose to watch porn over having sex is because they are feeling tired or lazy, not because they prefer it.
- Because sex is a bid for connection, sometimes when men are worried about being able to please or satisfy their partner, they may choose porn to avoid risking letting their female partner down or experiencing rejection.
- Despite watching porn, and sometimes choosing porn, men almost always indicate that they would *rather* have sex, as sex is about an intimate connection and not just a physical release.
- Consider porn the "canary in the coal mine"—a behavior that can be a helpful starting point for a conversation that can reveal pieces about your relational closeness and intimacy.

MYTH 6

The Desirability Myth

Dylan and Cindy had been together for almost ten years. They shared an interest in travel, art, and horror movies. They had twin daughters who had just turned three. The couple described themselves as very good friends who rarely fought. Overall things were happy and healthy. Well, that is, except for their sex life.

The couple said that sex in their relationship had always been somewhat nonexistent. Dylan said he had a pretty "healthy" sex drive but that Cindy had never shown much sexual interest. The couple had sex every few months at best, and when they did it wasn't that enjoyable. But now they felt it was time to see if there was *something* they could do to ignite a spark.

So I ask about the circumstances *around* sex—the dynamics outside of the bedroom that might be working for, or possibly against, the couple setting the mood.

Dylan said that he felt he had a high level of awareness of what Cindy needed in order to feel desired and cared for outside of the bedroom. He said he would take his time whenever they entered into a sexual scenario. That he would give her long massages to help her relax and ease into a romantic, sexual state. That he would tell her she looked beautiful. All the time. He would kiss her, buy her flowers, cook her dinner. He said he was doing everything he could think of to help get her in the mood and feel wanted.

I was about to shift to asking Cindy how those gestures made *her* feel when Dylan suddenly interrupted, "I just wish she would think about what I need for once!"

* * *

This chapter focuses on one of the biggest myths out there about men and sex: that is the belief in which women (and only women) are desirable while men (and only men) "do" the desiring. The myth that men don't need or even *want* to feel desirable. That feeling desirable simply doesn't matter to men. Because it's *men* who look at women. *Men* who notice women. And *men* who "chase" women. Certainly not the other way around.

And while research reliably documents that feeling desired is certainly an integral component of women's sexual desire, I will share some of the newest research, which suggests that men *also* want to be seen as sexy, desirable, and even *objectified* by their female partner. But because men's desire to feel desired challenges our social beliefs about men and sex, a lot of men don't voice how important this is to their experiences of sexual desire, and a lot of women don't think to outwardly demonstrate their desire for their male partners.

PEPÉ LE PEW AND PERCY SLEDGE

Girls are desirable. Boys do the desiring. At least that is what we've seen in popular culture since we were little children. And I do mean children. My earliest memory of this scenario comes from watching *The Bugs Bunny and Tweety Show* on Saturday mornings with my sister. Penelope, a female black cat, would accidentally and unknowingly get a stripe of white paint down her back and tail, making her appear like a skunk. Then Pepé Le Pew, an actual skunk, would saunter onto the screen, fall in love (or was it lust?), follow Penelope wherever she went, and try to serenade her with songs, flowers, poetry, and so forth. She ran, he chased.

His persistence seemed innocent and funny enough at the time. Although, as an adult, it's clear those "romantic" gestures were unwanted and the behavior was stalker-ish, creepy, and often flat-out harassment. But I digress . . .

The point is that from the youngest age possible, before we are even *thinking* about dating, sex, and romance, we received messages that suggest boys chase girls. Boys notice girls first. Men are enamored with a woman's beauty and make sure she knows it. He compliments her, buys her flowers and gifts, and invites her out for dinner. And *certainly* not the other way around.

This Pepé Le Pew story is hardly a random, outdated example. The reason this myth is held on to so tightly and widely is because it is reinforced early and often in many, many parts of our lives. Think, for example, about almost any classic love song. Eric Clapton wrote an entire ballad about how his wife looked "wonderful tonight." And he is far from being the only man to write a love song about the beauty of his female partner and how hard he is going to work to make her feel special. Think about Percy Sledge singing, "When a man loves a woman, he'll sleep out in the rain if that's the way she says it ought to be." Or George Harrison belting, "Something in the way she moves attracts me like no other lover." Or Elvis Presley belting, "I can't help falling in love with you." The list goes on and on. And on.

And as a woman I know how nice it can feel to listen to those songs. We can feel wanted. Not *necessarily* by Elvis or Eric or Percy or George (OK, *maybe* George . . . swoon!), but we might imagine a man we love or have a crush on feeling that way about *us*. We can imagine ourselves as the woman being wanted and desired and sway ourselves into a romantic dreamland.

In fact, any woman I've met or talked to, in my personal or professional life, has wanted to feel desired by the person she is intimately involved with. They light up when their partner tells them they look beautiful. They share photos on Instagram of the anniversary, birthday, or "just because" flowers their boyfriend or husband gave them. It's sweet. It's romantic. We feel special because we feel wanted, cared about, and desired. It just feels *good*.

It's not just receiving compliments about our appearances and small trinkets representing his affection. Think about how often, in our increasingly gender-parity society, that men are still picking up the check on a first date. Or how men save up to buy an expensive engagement ring for their fiancées (rarely with a gift in return, I might add). This pattern even follows us into the bedroom. Women, if the mood strikes, wear lacy bras and underwear or some form of lingerie. They are ultimately the desirable one while their male partners are the ones looking, desiring, lusting after them . . . most likely while adorned in some run-of-the-mill boxer briefs!

These social norms and expectations continually reinforce this one-sided pursuer-pursued relationship.

WOMEN'S DESIRE TO BE DESIRED

> "It's a like a huge aphrodisiac for women, to feel like their partners want them because it makes them feel sexy and desired."—Chelsea, age twenty-seven

As this quote highlights, men making women feel desired isn't just something that *happens*—it's something that (in the context of consensual, healthy loving relationships) feels really, really good for most women.

There are *plenty* of ways that women can feel desired. Women may feel wanted by their partner when he brings home a box of her favorite macaroons "just because." Or when he tells her how good she looks when stepping into the shower. Or the feeling she gets when he picks up the tab on a night out like it was a first date (even if you have a shared bank account now!). Whatever the preference, my research suggests that women like when their male partner makes his desire for her known, whether it be through physical touch, longing looks, or just flat out saying it.[1] Here are a few examples:

> "If he is showing that he is really attracted to me, either verbally or physically, then that will trigger [desire] for me."

> "That's definitely a turn on, knowing that your partner wants you and actually makes it known. Whether it's, like, saying it or, if we're together, like if he touches me."

> "Yeah, he constantly is trying to fondle me, so that makes me feel desire. Mainly because it makes me feel good and confident and it makes me feel good about myself. Sometimes he'll watch me change or try to get in the shower with me, that that'll make me feel good. So then I obviously feel the desire to have sex."

On the other hand, when women feel that their partner is *not* making his desire for her explicitly known, it seems to have the opposite effect.[2] That is, a *lack* of feeling desired seems to decrease women's sexual desire and can contribute to a less-than-satisfying sex life. As one woman I spoke with described, "I feel like if he were to make an effort to kiss me passionately or come up and say something to me, like express that he has desire for me, then I'd probably get turned on. But he doesn't do that."

WINE AND DINE

But, as any woman knows all too well, our sexual desire is not so surface level that if our male partners simply walks up to us and grab our butts or give us a sultry look that we topple into bed with lust! Feeling desired also includes gestures that occur *around* sex. Like when our partners are sensitive, caring, thoughtful, and romantic. In fact, women in my research have often described that when their partners seduce them *outside* of a sexual setting, it makes them more likely to want to engage in sexual activity later on. For example,

> "There are specific things he can do to put me in the mood. Like sometimes he'll cook me a really nice dinner and he'll do something really cheesy romantic, which he doesn't do often, you know? Like he'll light some candles or he'll dim the lights in the bedroom and have the bedroom all set up or something."

Cooking a special dinner is just one example of what can help some women feel desired because it is a tangible example of feeing cared about. You can *see* the effort. And for many women this type of gesture makes them feel special and wanted. It's like non-erotic foreplay. It might not get the juices flowing to have sex in the kitchen right then and there, but it can be the start of a slow burning flame that builds over the course of the evening. As another participant I spoke with described, it's the effort that matters more than the dinner itself:

> "It just shows that he's planned something or that he put thought into what's going on instead of rolling over in bed and saying 'Hey, what's going on?' like it just feels like it's more thought put into it and I think that's what I appreciate more."

On the other hand, women who find their partners just initiate sex out of the blue, without any romance or build up, without any feeling of being desired by their partner throughout the day, tend to have a more difficult time leading into sex.[3] Another woman I spoke with said,

> "When it comes down to it, when you're hopping into bed at night and there has been no romance throughout the day, for me, I'm like 'Back off, you can't just expect that right away.'"

Women all have different examples of what makes them feel desirable— whether it's a "*Damn*, you look good" comment before heading out to a social gathering, being touched in *that* way, or thoughtful gestures that make them feel seen and appreciated, the feeling of being wanted, desired, and cared about regularly and reliably is described as being integral to women's experiences of sexual desire.

IT'S ALL ABOUT THE MONEY?

Ladies: have you ever thought to yourself as you strutted by your partner, "I wonder if he thinks I look sexy?" or "I think I'm turning him on"?

If you have, then you have a glimpse into what sex researchers Dr. Lori Brotto and Dr. Anthony Bogeart term *object of desire self-consciousness*.[4] It's the idea that our sexuality and our desirability are intrinsically interconnected with what men think about our sexuality and desirability. Drs. Brotto and Boegart specifically suggest that heterosexual women have internalized ideas about what heterosexual men find attractive and then we evaluate our own appearance against those norms. How close (or far away) we are to meeting those norms results in our internal evaluations of our attractiveness and desirability. So if we perceive that someone else finds us sexy, we tend to think of ourselves as a little sexier, too. On the other hand, if we perceive that others see us as *unattractive*, we take on that perception and feel less attractive.

For example, if we believe that men are attracted to curvy women with big breasts and shapely behinds and we see ourselves as flat chested and waif-like, we will feel somewhat unattractive and unsexy in comparison. In contrast, if we believe that men like women with big pouty lips and we happen to have big pouty lips (naturally or with the use of some strategic lipstick), we may internalize ourselves as being sexy and desirable.

The key thing, according to this theory, is that how good we feel, how sexy we feel, and how *desirable* we feel is completely intertwined with how good, sexy, and desirable women perceive we are to someone else. It goes without saying that this is a pretty precarious way for women to arrive at their sexual self-evaluations and it has some notable drawbacks. With the degree to which women's bodies have been objectified to sell cars, hamburgers, perfume, fashion, and anything in between, it can be degrading and harmful at worst, and fodder for insecurity at best. These are big and important issues, to be sure, but beyond the scope of this particular book. What *is* within the scope of this book is whether men need to feel desired too and whether they want, or need, their desirability to be reinforced by the woman they are in a relationship with.

Theoretically speaking it has been proposed that while women evaluate their desirability based on others' evaluations of their *physical appearance*, men's internalization of their desirability is more about their *behavior*.[5] Specifically, men's desirability is thought to be based on their dominance, whether that be socially (e.g., the leader of the pack), professionally (e.g., the newly named legal partner), or athletically (e.g., the star football player), and their resources, such as their possessions (e.g., a high-end car) and income (e.g., having a six-figure salary).

Let's consider the fictional character Don Draper. Picture his powerful strut; his deep, raspy negotiation voice; his perfectly tailored gray suit; and his confident sexy stare while he sips his Manhattan. Now, according to the object of desire self-consciousness theory, Mr. Draper might be considered desirable (and he might consider himself a catch) because of his prestigious and high-paying job on Madison Avenue, his nice car, and fancy suit. It shows he can provide. And according to evolutionary-based theories, these are cues for a woman that a man can take care of her (and perhaps even their future child). So it *should* be attractive. And in some ways it certainly is.

But what if men actually want to feel desired for how they look, too? What if men want their female partner to see beyond what they have and see just who they are? What if men actually do care about how they look and want to know that their female partner sees it, too?

I'M TOO SEXY

I want to start by sharing some of the messages I've heard from men in my research about how their physical appearance actually *do* matter.

Specifically, some men I spoke with described needing to feel that they were attractive, sexy, and worthy of being involved in a sexual encounter. Feeling sexy was something men described as an internal self-evaluation. A feeling that was related to their own self-esteem and feelings of self-worth. As an example, take a look at what one participant described when I asked him about his ideal sexual experience—and how it's his own evaluation of his attractiveness (i.e., whether he feels sexy) that is critical to his sexual desire:

> "If we're talking about sexual desire in an ideal setting, I'm also feeling quite confident and attractive, right? Because I find, since we've had kids and I'm not taking care of myself as much as I used to, and I've gained a bit of weight and all that stuff that comes along with turning forty, I find it's not as rich an experience as it used to be when I was going to university and lifting weights and eating well and I was active. So I felt sexy."

Men also described the importance of feeling attractive and sexy in the sense that if they did *not* feel this good, they were not interested in having sex. For example, having a cold or feeling tired were described as examples of times men might feel less sexy and attractive and, thus, not in the mood for sex. For example, "If you're not feeling well or if you have a cold you obviously don't feel like being intimate because I don't think you feel attractive." And another participant shared,

> "I feel less sexy when I'm tired . . . if I'm in an in-between state of tiredness, I'll feel, although my sex drive is still there, I will feel that I'm undesirable. And I'll feel I will feel less sexy even knowing that sexual feelings are still around. I'll feel like I wouldn't be able to do a good job of having sex anyway."

Further, men in my research were not impervious to experiencing insecurities with regard to their body image, as some societal norms might suggest. Some men described feeling that if they were having a less confident day, comparing their body to other men or considering how they perceived their overall masculinity, they felt less sexual desire. The following participant described a circumstance in which he did not feel desire:

"When I'm having a really down day, low confidence, that's when it really hits me . . . you know? Even in terms of body image. . . . Those messages that you're not big enough, you're not sexy enough, you're not top dog enough."

These findings suggest that wanting to feel sexy and wanting to look good is a reality for a lot more men than we tend to realize. In fact this finding has been replicated in other research on men's sexual arousal as well,[6] but hasn't been picked up by mainstream media in the same way findings that support our stereotypes about men and women tend to.

MALIBU KEN DOLL

This may sound initially counterintuitive, but here's a quick story about some pushback I once got to this idea about men caring about their looks and wanting to look sexy. I was presenting my research and was getting a lot of questions and interest about the idea that men want to feel desired. There were lots of positive comments, but one man in the room questioned the importance of men's physical appearance. He suggested that most men didn't care so much about their appearance. Perhaps they care about their financial and power status, but not about their looks. Maybe, he thought, I was interpreting my data wrong?

I remember being thrown for a loop because I was so *in* my data, so *in* the mentality that men's desire to be desired was *critically* important to their sexuality that I forgot others hadn't had the same epiphany as I had. That this finding may challenge some people's ideas about men and it could take some time to digest. I began doubting myself for a moment, wondering if maybe the men I spoke with were the minority or if I was perhaps overstating a fact. Because when you're a woman telling a room full of people about men's desire and a *man* disagrees with you, it can be pretty unsettling!

But after my presentation I was in the bathroom and noticed a poster. It was a shaving brand that had six different men with different stylized beards. The clean-shaven man, the slightly manicured (but not too manicured!) lumberjack beard, the goatee, the really thin chinstrap, and so on. And my jaw dropped. I thought, "Wait a second! Isn't this *exactly* what we were just talking about? An ad targeting men who care very much about their appearance? Isn't this the *exact* type of advertisement that would have typically targeted *women* in the past? The 'Which kind of woman do you want to be?' question? Are you nerdy Barbie? Scientist Barbie? Teacher Barbie? Wasn't this, in fact, a de facto 'Which kind of Ken Doll do you want to be?'"

And this poster is part of a larger narrative about men's appearances that have been happening, but just enough under the surface to be kind of ignored, for quite some time.

HE'S *SO* METROSEXUAL

Remember the term *metrosexual*? It sounds so outdated now. And that's because it kind of is. This word became trendy in the midnineties to reflect the growing number of heterosexual men who cared about their fashion choices and appearance.[7] Actually, let me put that another way— it was a word used to reflect the growing number of heterosexual men who *felt comfortable* putting effort into their fashion choices and appearance. But as a society we apparently needed a word to make sure it was clear they weren't homosexual. Because up until that point we believed it was only gay men who cared about that kind of stuff. So metrosexual became in vogue. Heterosexual men who landscaped (a.k.a. man-scaped) their bodies, wore designer clothing, and did so with pride.

Why am I delving into this history lesson? Well, to illustrate a point: although some of us still like to think that men just don't care about their appearance and what they look like, in actuality this has been occurring for quite some time. And I'm not in any way trying to suggest that men caring about their appearance only started occurring twenty-odd years ago! This is hardly a millennial or generation X thing!

I'm not a historian but if we look even further back there have been plenty of instances when men clearly put a lot of effort into their appearances. Think about the bright and shiny (sometimes outright revealing) disco outfits of the seventies. The product "greasers" used to style their hair just right in the fifties. The high-top hats made of expensive silky beaver felt in the 1800s. All I'm saying is that if you start looking, men are (and have been) spending a great deal of time and effort on their physical appearance, their hair, their clothing, their bodies. And maybe, *just maybe*, they want their female partner to notice?

I WANT YOU TO WANT ME

Cue the girls shrieking, the drumbeat, and the electric guitar slide. This Cheap Trick song might have *appealed* to a female crowd, but consider this: they are an *all-male* band, singing from *their* perspective. I want *you* to want me. I *need* you to need me.

When I interviewed men for my research, I just wanted to know more about what impacted men's desire. I didn't go in with any particular ideas or expectations. But interview after interview it started to become very clear that the most salient and important experience that increased men's sexual desire was feeling wanted by their female partner. Not to other women walking down the street, at work, or at the club, but to their girlfriend or their wife. For example, as one man I spoke to described wanting to feel desirable to his girlfriend, "She understands that's important to me, to feel that I'm very desirable to her. Like, particularly to her."

And while most men I've spoken with describe that being desired was important to their experience of sexual desire, there was also an awareness that this was a rare and unusual occurrence. That socially there was a belief that women want or need to feel desired while men "do the wanting." That being said, men described the desire to be desired as being a universal need among both men and women:

> "I think it's a basic human need. I don't think you can distinguish between men and women. The reality is everyone wants to be desired. Everyone wants to be connected. From a man's point of view, from my point of view, there is a very strong connection and a need to be wanted . . . there has to be a connection, there has to be a need to be wanted to the point where you feel as though they need you as much as you need them."

So then, what does feeling desired look like for men? There are three key things that have stood out to me over the course of my research and clinical practice. I'll discuss each in turn.

1. You Are *So* Good Looking

As much as many men care about their physical appearance and feeling sexy as a self-evaluation, they also want to hear that their female partner finds them attractive. Some of men I talked with indicated that when they received compliments from their partners (or sometimes women in general), they felt desired. And that felt really good. Men perceived compliments about their attractiveness or overall worthiness as a sexual partner to be the most meaningful. As an example, when asked about the most memorable experience of sexual desire he had experienced in the last year, one participant shared a memory of when he was grocery shopping with his wife; she later told him that he had caught her (and her friend's) eye among the other men in the crowd. He said,

> "There was one specific time where she had indicated she had seen me at a farmer's market among a whole bunch of people, and just the way I was dressed and the other person commented that she thought I looked very hot. And not hot in the sense of being warm. And this was in the summer time. And I hadn't heard a positive comment or a compliment in a long time. So that triggered for me that there was a noticeable comment. There was a reflection that I was desired."

Another man described a similar experience of memorable, heightened sexual desire when he overheard two women at work talking about his desirable attributes, not only sexually, but also as a partner in general. Although, in this example, the compliments came from women outside of his relationship, the participant described the experience as one that increased his desire to be with his wife, because he had confidence that he was *worth* desiring. He said,

> "It would have to be a couple times when I got a compliment or something at work. It didn't even increase my sexual desire for that person at all. But that in and of itself seemed very empowering. Kind of like, knowing that someone else had a physical attraction towards me built up that sexual desire. And it was almost like I wanted to go home and say a 'Honey, I'm home!' kind of thing. Just feel that empowerment."

Men indicated that it felt so good to receive compliments, suggesting that while women appear to receive compliments all the time, men also would enjoy receiving this attention but do so less often. He said,

> "[Women] get adored quite a bit more to the point where they feel very, sometimes feel extra good about themselves. And start feeling like very sexual beings because they get these compliments and getting

the little 'woo-hoos' or whatever. And most men don't get that very often. And when they do, it's pretty darn good."

In other words men seem to want to experience some validation and affirmation about their physical appearance. As I previously described, men seem to care more about their physical appearance than we might have acknowledged. They want to feel *sexy* in order to want to have sex. And while this is partially an internal evaluation, receiving compliments from female partners helps elucidate this feeling.

2. Women's Sexual Interest

Feeling desired for men isn't *just* through verbal affirmations. In the same way that we explored the ways that many women like to feel desired through words, touch, and gestures, men have a similar (but different) trifecta of desirability.

When it comes to nonverbal signs of desire, men in my research indicated that there was a feeling they had when their female partner was engaged and present for the sexual activity that made them feel *wanted*. It seemed to be almost an intangible experience: something that men just "knew" or could sense. When men got this feeling they described it as a huge aphrodisiac—primarily because it made them feel desired in return. One man I spoke with shared: "If I think you're reluctantly going along with me, it doesn't make me feel like you're participating. I need you to participate for me to feel wanted, loved, desired." I particularly love that quote because he lists three words as if they are synonymous: wanted, loved, and desired. And based on what I've learned about men and sex, I can say that that is certainly not a coincidence.

Perceiving a female partner's sexual interest was described as having a very positive impact on men's sexual desire. As a couple of other men shared, "I enjoy the sexual part of a marriage or relationship. So I think when you find someone . . . showing interest, it excites you even more. So it spikes the desire." And another: "It would be kind of revitalizing. If I was tired and . . . my wife, is interested in me, well she's really into me tonight. That's awesome."

Over the course of my research men unanimously indicated that they had no interest in having sex with a woman who was not an equal, interested, and enthusiastic partner (which should come as no surprise since reading the chapter The Selfish Myth). Rather they described having a strong spike in sexual desire when their female partner showed an interest in having sex with them. When their partners appeared to be interested in having sex, men described feeling more desired, more confident, and reassured that their interest in shared sexual activity was mutual.

3. She Started It

Receiving compliments and being able to perceive their partner's genuine interest in engaging in sexual activity are important to many men's sexual desire. However, the majority of men I have spoken with indicate that the most significant evidence of their partner's desire for them was when she initiated sexual activity. Here are a few men putting this in their own words:

> "It's one thing for your partner to say they want you. But to have them physically initiate and do it is another."

> "If she does initiate it or suggest it, absolutely that's great. She wants to have sex. It doesn't take me long if she's in that kind of mood."

> "If my partner wanted to initiate something I'd be right there."

Having a female partner initiate sexual activity is exciting for a few interconnected reasons. First, it tends to be described as a somewhat rare occurrence, which made it seem more exciting, new, and different. Second, when a female partner initiates sex, it also allays men's fears about rejection (which we will explore more in The Rejection Myth chapter). This quote from Matthew highlights the connection between initiation and fear of rejection:

> "It's very exciting when all of a sudden she wants it. When she's making the motions for it, and she is asking for it, and she is actually the one who initiates everything. Um, that is so far and few between with her that, yeah, it's exciting. When I'm not the one who has to do all the work. When I'm not the one who has to worry about getting rejected."

The desire to be desired was the most critical, common, and significant elicitor of sexual desire described by men in my research. Men I've spoken with have made it so abundantly clear that their sexual desire (and even their self-esteem and self-worth) are strongly enhanced when they received reassurance of their female partner's desire for him. Whether it was receiving compliments, their female partners showing an interest during sexual activity, or—the ultimate form of desirability—when their female partner *initiated* sexual activity (which just so happens to be the focus of our next chapter!). The desire to be desired has been highlighted reliably and regularly over the course of my research with men.

WHY THIS MYTH IS A PROBLEM

The myth that men don't need to feel desired—and that they are the ones to just "do the wanting"—presents a problem for both men and women. Simply speaking, believing in this myth creates an uneven playing ground in heterosexual relationships. At best it places a great deal of responsibility on the man's shoulders and takes sexual agency and responsibility *off* of the woman's shoulders. And at worst it reinforces a toxic unidirectional dynamic in which women are objectified by men instead of realizing we *all* want to feel wanted and desired in our own ways (balanced with times where we may want to *do* the desiring—or even objectifying).

Women: When is the last time you told your partner he looked good? I mean *really* told him. Explicitly. Enough that he heard you and said thanks?

As we have explored throughout this chapter, because it runs counter to the messages we receive incessantly throughout our lives, most women simply don't think about complimenting their husband's or boyfriend's appearance because we have been raised to think it doesn't matter all that much to them. But a little bit of praise can go a long way. So the next time you're going out on a nice date or to a party, notice whether your husband compliments your dress, your hair, or just generally how you look. And then pay attention to whether you said anything back to him—even just "Nice suit" or "That tie really brings out your eyes."

Consider sharing that you thought he looked really good in that baby blue sweater the other day. Or that you've noticed he's been working out or shaved or *whatever*. Buy him a small gift or trinket that you think he would like. Something that shows him you were thinking about him. Find what feels right to you and what he might appreciate and then just *do it*. These types of gestures keep the intimate wheel turning in relationships. If there is a one-sided dynamic (and you can insert any example here: cooking dinner, cleaning the kitchen, making the bed, taking out the garbage, etc.), we tend to tire of putting in effort.

Making your partner feel desirable isn't just an altruistic gesture. There is an upside for you in positively reinforcing your partner's physical appearance when appropriate. Namely? Chances are he will feel good when you do it and he may put in a little more effort into *his* physical appearance. I can't tell you how many times I hear couples talk about how hard it is to feel motivated to have sex if they are sitting around in their pajamas. "Netflix and chill" becomes a *literal* Netflix and chill. But notice what happens if you tell your partner that he looks good when he keeps his suit or work clothes on when he gets home. Or at least if he changes into jeans versus sweats. I'm not a betting woman, but I feel confident suggesting that giving enough of those compliments will increase his efforts to dress and present himself nicely. So positively reinforcing the effort *he* puts into his physical appearance may just circle back to increase your own interest in having sex.

Men: As with anything that you would like to experience more of in your relationship, it's about accepting the behaviors and providing positive reinforcement. If you *like* when your girlfriend tells you that you look good, mention that. She certainly won't keep it up if you brush it off and try to act too dismissive—or say, "Yeah, whatever." *Embrace* that you care (to whatever degree) about your appearance. It's normal and it's important. It's OK—even advisable—to take some pride in how you present yourself when you're at home. Maybe don't put on those sweatpants or pajamas right away.

Separate from your appearance, if there is a time where your girlfriend did something specific that made you feel desirable (whether that was complimenting you in front of your friends, rubbing your back while you were cooking, or remembering your favorite five-spice chili recipe), tell her it made you feel good. She might not know that it made you feel wanted and desired. Risk it. Open up. Tell her.

Also, know how important it is for you to continue expressing your desire for her, *even* if you wish more gestures were coming your way in return. The more you keep it up, the more likely she will be to reciprocate (or, at minimum, you can use those examples to help her see what you're doing to help *her* feel desired and suggest it might be nice to see that effort going both ways). In addition, ask yourself about how you're showing your desire and whether it's what *she* really likes. You might *think* she likes it when you tell her she looks sexy getting into the shower—but she might feel busy, rushed, and even self-conscious if she's not in a sexy headspace. Instead she might feel more desired when you give her a compliment about her appearance when she is getting ready to go out with her girlfriends and can let the compliment sink in. Don't assume you know. Ask.

MYTH IN ACTION: DYLAN AND CINDY

The Case of the One-Way Street

Dylan and Cindy were on different pages about what they wanted from the sexual part of their relationship. Dylan said he wanted sex ideally once a week but Cindy said she could take or leave it. As a result they "compromised" by having sex about once every few months. So they came to see me to see if there was a chance to better understand Cindy's desire (or lack thereof) and possibly improve their sexual interactions. Then Dylan made that comment about feeling he was trying to please Cindy but didn't feel like she was focusing on his needs in return.

So I asked him to say a bit more. Dylan indicated that he felt he put so much time and effort into helping Cindy get in the mood—he catered to her needs, pulled back when she wanted him to, only had sex on "her schedule"—and although she was willing to have sex on those rare occasions, even then he did not feel that she was really into it. He said that he just wished that she would think about what he needed sometimes. And on top of that he said he watched her day in and day out cuddle, snuggle, and kiss their daughters. She paid so much attention to these little children. He could see she had affection to give, but it wasn't in his direction.

Cindy was pretty surprised to hear this. Dylan was a people pleaser. Up until now in the relationship he had never expressed any signs of frustration about putting in all this effort. She said she had no idea he felt this way. We asked Dylan to say a bit more so she could understand where he was coming from.

What did Dylan want? He said he didn't want kinky sex, he didn't care if Cindy wore lingerie, and he certainly didn't want her to have sex with him every day. He just wanted her to see and appreciate him for what he did *beyond* work around the house. Although he said Cindy would say thank you when he shoveled the driveway, took out the garbage, cleaned, and so on, he wished she could give him the same appreciation for *him*, not doing anything. Just for being him. Notice when he got a haircut, check him out sometimes when he was changing. Compliment his body when he was working out. Compliment him for just being *him*.

Cindy took this to heart. She didn't have much of an interest in sex, but she did appreciate Dylan and she still found him attractive. Cindy said she would try to tell him more often when she noticed when he looked cute. To pay a bit more attention to the little things like when he got a haircut or a new shirt. We agreed there was more work to be done to understand Cindy's lower interest in having sex, but for the time being the couple would work on embracing and exchanging their desire for one another *outside* of the bedroom. And Dylan said that those changes made a noticeable difference to him. Feeling desired by Cindy again made some of the stretches between sex a little more manageable.

SUMMARY

Feeling sexually desirable may be more integral to men's experiences of sexual desire than we tend to recognize or acknowledge.

- Societal messages, from our childhood and throughout our adult lives, regularly and reliably depict men desiring and lusting after women, and rarely the other way around.
- Feeling sexually desired is a significant component of women's experiences of sexual desire.
- Women report feeling desired through words, touch, and romantic thoughtful gestures that make them feel seen and appreciated.
- Men's experience of desirability is more complex than appreciation of status, wealth, and possessions.
- Men's physical appearance, specifically feeling confident and sexy, is important to men's ability to feel sexual desire.

- Men report wanting to feel desired through receiving compliments as well as sensing their partner's enjoyment of sexual activity and female sexual initiation.
- When men and women each take an active role in desiring *and* being desired, it allows for a more egalitarian relationship and promotes increased sexual passion.

MYTH 7

The Initiation Myth

Courtney was finally feeling in the mood to have sex. It had been a long week. She and her boyfriend Dave hadn't had a chance to talk much, let alone connect intimately. But now her work deadline had been met, her stress was temporarily on hold, and she felt relaxed and ready to let her hair down.

So after dinner, when Dave was sitting on the couch watching the news, instead of sitting on the other couch, as she might otherwise, Courtney came and sat down right beside him.

Dave looked at her, gave her a smile, and went back to watching TV.

They sat together like that for a little while and then Courtney rested her head on Dave's shoulder and nestled in a bit closer to him.

Dave put his hand on her leg, gave her a kiss on her forehead, and went back to watching the news.

Courtney was feeling confused and a little bit disheartened and thought, "Come on, Dave! What are you waiting for? Make a move already!" Except that she didn't say those words out loud, and he didn't make a move. They just continued to watch TV and eventually went to bed, with Courtney feeling emotionally, and very sexually, frustrated.

Later that week, when the couple was in my office, I asked about whether there had been any sexual interactions since our last session. When they reported that they had not had sex since we last met, Courtney said, "It's not *my* fault we didn't have sex. I wanted to have sex on Saturday but *you* didn't make a move."

"What!?" Dave said as he threw his arms up in the air. "If you wanted to have sex why didn't you tell me!?"

* * *

In this chapter we'll break down the most prevalent sexual interaction pattern that occurs in heterosexual relationships. That is, *he* initiates sexual activity and *she* says yes or no. This sexual pattern is *so* deeply ingrained in our sexual experiences that we rarely pause to question what impact it has on our sexual satisfaction. Unfortunately, the fact that this is the most *likely* dynamic that precedes sexual activity does not mean it is in any way optimal for our relationships.

The myth that men *should* initiate sexual activity stems from two other myths we have already debunked in this book. The first is the *gender myth*: the myth that men want more sex than women so they should be the one to push or ask for it. The second is the *desirability myth*: the myth that men just do the wanting and don't need to feel romanced or desired in return. But as we now know, men are *just* as likely as women to have the higher sex drive in an intimate relationship and they *do* want to feel wanted and "chased." This chapter is going expand on those two myths and hone in on sexual initiation directly. We will explore *how* we came to hold the belief that men should initiate sex, *why* more and more men are keen to forego the responsibility and limiting gender norms that come with initiating all (or the vast majority of) sex, and *how* a more egalitarian sexual initiation pattern can increase sexual satisfaction and women's sexual agency.

ONLY ABOUT THAT THING

It's one of those things that we just intuitively *know*: men are most often the ones who initiate sex while women say yes or no. Theoretical models of heterosexual relationship based on years of observations assert this fact.[1] And, better than that, the theory holds up to empirical research. For example, in one of my studies of over two hundred male participants (age eighteen to sixty-five) in relationships, almost two-thirds (63 percent) of men indicated that they initiated almost exclusively or significantly more often than their female partner. Similarly, in a qualitative study with thirty-two male participants (age eighteen to twenty-five) about men's engagement in, and preference for, various patterns of sexual initiation, Dr. Shari Dworkin and Dr. Lucia O'Sullivan concluded that male-dominated sexual initiation was by far the most common pattern of initiation.[2] This finding was also replicated in another more recent qualitative study of forty-four men (age eighteen to twenty-five).[3] Just to name a few examples.

But before we go any further I want to pause to address the question: *why* do the majority of us participate in this dominant pattern in which men initiate sex and women say yes or no? Well, the sexual initiation patterns that exist in heterosexual relationships stem from messages we received *long* before we ever met our partner. How far back exactly? Just think about some of the first messages we learned about sex when we were teenagers.

Teenage girls are taught early, and often, to value and *protect* their sexuality. They are told that they shouldn't share their bodies with just *anyone*; they should be selective. Girls learn to be skeptical about boys' intentions, because they are warned boys are only looking for "one thing." They want *sex*. They probably don't care about you. So girls are told to make sure they wait until they find someone they *love* before having sex. In other words girls are taught to be on the lookout for sexual advances from boys and to turn down their sexual proposals. And young women most certainly do not learn to embrace or seek out sex. That's the antithesis of what a "good girl" does! Essentially women were told to be what is referred to as the gatekeeper—the one who says yes (but, preferably no) to sexual advances from boys.

Now, teenage boys are a different story. Most men are warned about sex at least when it comes to unwanted pregnancies and sexually transmitted infections and diseases (I don't think any of us got a hall pass on those slideshows from the public health nurse!). But most young men are not discouraged from being sexual or encouraged to wait until they fall in love to have sex. In contrast, young men sometimes receive some form of affirmation (or perhaps more accurately, pressure) from their peers if they are able to have sex (more on that when we get to the *masculinity myth*). So men learned to push for sexual activity, to be the one to suggest sex or initiate sex, all to increase their chances of getting laid.

Taken together, most men in our society were taught to *pursue* and seek out sex, while women were taught to say no and play hard to get.

And this message about men initiating sex and women gatekeeping doesn't just magically disappear when we enter into a relationship. In committed partnerships, men still are more often the ones to suggest sex in some way. *He's* the one to playfully pat his girlfriend's butt when he walks by her in the hallway. *He's* the one to start moving in closer when slow dancing in the kitchen. *He's* the one who slides his hand up her leg while cuddling on the couch. And then *she* decides, "Hmm, yeah, that feels good. Let's go with it" or "What on earth is he thinking? This is clearly the worst time ever!" and he stops.

In short, *he* knocks at her door, and *she* decides whether or not to let him in.[4]

WHOSE LINE IS IT ANYWAY?

What I just outlined is the basis for what sociologists refer to as a sexual script.[5] Sexual scripts are a form of social script—a set of guidelines or rules that we use to help navigate interactions in the world around us.[6] The word *script* was intentionally and appropriately chosen because it highlights how we are essentially acting out a play, each reading from our lines. First you say A, then I say B, then we both do C.

Social scripts happen in almost every interaction we encounter. Take, for example, when you order a latte at your favorite coffee shop. The scene starts with you waiting your turn in line, deciding on your order. Then the barista calls you to the till. You tell her you would like a grande chai tea latte, please and thank you. The barista asks if you want something sweet to go with it. You say yes, that birthday cake pop looks delicious (or, I suppose, if you have any self-control you say no). Then she asks how you're paying. You tap your debit card. Then you stand to the side until the barista calls your name and hands you your drink with your name scribbled incorrectly on the cup.

For the most part, these scripts are helpful blueprints for how we behave socially. If we didn't have them, social interactions would feel pretty confusing. We all know that feeling when someone *isn't* playing by the rules (or perhaps doesn't know them). They cut in line, take too long mulling over their order, order a medium instead of a grande, or talk loudly on their phone and don't hear the barista calling their name when their order is up.

Whether it's a guest walking into your house and opening your fridge before you offer them food; the "too cool" kid who walks into class late, stoned, and doesn't respect the teacher; or the first timer at a poetry jam who cheers loudly instead of snapping their fingers, it just feels *wrong* when someone isn't following the script. "What are you doing?!" we think to ourselves. "We're all playing by the rules here. You can't do *that!*"

What I'm saying is that *generally speaking* these scripts offer us context, and a sense of what to expect when we interact with others. And we don't like it when people deviate from them. But, as *we* grow and change our scripts need to keep up. There are times where we may find some of our social, and sexual, scripts just aren't working so well. And it's time to question whether we might need to create a *new* and better script.

BREAKING THE RULES

Just because *most* men and women report participating in the dominant pattern of male-led sexual initiation doesn't mean that we *want* to play by these rules. In my first set of interviews with men about their sexual desire it was common to hear them describe their frustrations with having to bear the brunt of the initiation load.[7] For example, Jessie shared with me that even when his female partner was the one who wanted to have sex, or suggested it in some subtle way, he was still expected to initiate. If he missed her signs she would often tell him it was too late, that the time had passed. Something he obviously found quite frustrating:

> "Even when she wants sex she'll still expect me to initiate. . . . I'll get home and give her a kiss and she'll say, 'why didn't we have sex in the morning? We can't have it now,' and I'm like 'Well, why didn't you roll over and . . . if you really wanted sex why didn't you let me know?'"

I've also interviewed men who describe feeling *pressure* to initiate sex even when they aren't in the mood for sex. They have described how the expectation that *men* initiate sex is so strong that they almost do it on command, without thinking about whether they really want it. One of my interviewees, Bruce, described how he initiated sex with his wife almost every night and then she would say yes or no. And he admitted he often didn't feel desire for sex but still played along with their "little game." When I asked what would happen if he *didn't* initiate sex on a night he wasn't in the mood for, Bruce responded,

> "She'd notice if I wasn't doing it that way. I almost have to do it to kind of keep up appearances to some extent. She would think something was wrong if I wasn't desiring her . . . that I wasn't acting like myself or I was upset with her."

Despite sexual scripts being so deeply ingrained, there is increasing evidence that they are starting to shift.[8] In the qualitative study I described earlier, Dworkin and O'Sullivan asked not only *what* men's current sexual initiation patterns looked like, but also what they *wanted* them to look like. That is, they wanted to know how congruent men's current sexual initiation patterns were with their *preferred* initiation patterns. And while most men indicated that they were primarily responsible for sexual initiation, the majority of the men (72.2 percent) indicated that they would *prefer* a more egalitarian pattern of initiation. That is, they wanted equal amounts of initiation between themselves and their female partner.[9] Essentially the men in this study described that being primarily responsible for initiating sex was "too demanding" and they rejected the idea of a dichotomous male/female script (i.e., the belief that because I'm a man I do *X* and because you're a woman you do *Y*).[10]

Similarly, 60 percent of the men in my research said they would *prefer* that their female partner initiate sex more regularly. The responses ranged from anything like "I would prefer it was 50/50" to "It would be nice if she initiated for once." And, notably, the second largest response in my study—the men who said the initiation pattern was fine the way things were (14 percent)—*already* reported that their female partner initiated somewhat frequently or even equally to them. So no matter how you cut it, *most* men would like to be initiating sex a little less and having their female partner initiate a little bit (and sometimes a lot) more.

SHUT UP AND KISS ME

If you've ever read a sexual health magazine, relationship advice column, or sex blog, you've *probably* received the message loud and clear that men love it when women initiate sexual activity. The suggestion is usual-

ly that men find it really sexy when women approach them out of no-
where, by wearing something really sexy (or nothing at all) or by grabbing them below the belt.

And to be fair, there are times where this could be *precisely* what men
want. As Jordan described, he just wanted his girlfriend to surprise him at
random by grabbing him: "I would like her to initiate more. And more
importantly, at unexpected (but appropriate) times. Watching TV? Don't
need to say anything; just take my cock out. I'm brushing my teeth?
Come up behind me and grab my crotch."

But as you know by now, this book goes far beyond those tired clichés
about the most important thing to men's sexuality being unexpected blow
jobs. I will argue that the reason many men want their female partner to
initiate more (and he wants to initiate less) is more complex and relational
than most of us tend to acknowledge.

CELEBRITY CRUSH NUMBER 3

Let me start by telling you about another of my top celebrity crushes
(along with John Krasinski and George Harrison if you're keeping track):
Canadian mega babe Ryan Reynolds. Recently I was watching the movie
Just Friends starring my imaginary boyfriend and the funny and charming Amy Smart. Ryan Reynolds plays a geeky, overweight teenager who
is in love with his much more attractive best (girl) friend all throughout
high school. Later in life they reconnect and she realizes she has feelings
for him. The peak of the movie is this scene where *she* is trying to give
him signs that she is interested in hooking up. She suggests they have a
sleepover (just like old times when they were . . . wait for it . . . *just
friends*). She puts on his oversized dress shirt and lingers in the bathroom
doorway suggestively. She gets into bed with him and gives him a look.
Then she says her feet are cold and asks if they could snuggle. All along
you hear the inner dialogue of Ryan Reynolds's character, who is trying
to get up the guts to make a move. But as the scene goes on he just gets
more and more nervous. He is debilitated and unable to make a move, so
he does nothing but say good night. She is left deflated, and he's mad at
himself for missing the opportunity. The next day she says to a friend that
she can't believe nothing happened; "I was essentially throwing myself at
him!"

That scene highlights what so many sexual interactions look like between men and women. *She* feels like she is basically throwing herself at him but he's thinking, "Wait, what if I'm misreading? What if I make a move and she actually isn't in the mood? That would be so awkward and embarrassing."

If you're thinking, "OK, fine. But this movie depicts a couple who weren't *really* a couple. Of course it's harder to read the signs in that situation than it would be in a committed relationship with someone you know well." It's a reasonable thought. Except that it's not the case.

MEN *STILL* CAN'T READ THE SIGNS?

It turns out that men who are dating, and even *married* to, their female partner sometimes still have a difficult time reading the signs that she's in the mood (remember that study from The Gender Myth chapter?)[11] and, at times, men describe being uncertain about whether their partner is initiating sex. (There is a good reason for this, but we'll wait to unpack it in the next chapter: The Rejection Myth.)

In fact, men consistently indicate that they would prefer that their female partner could be clearer and more explicit about initiating sex when she is doing it so that he knows exactly what she wants. As Hart said, "I wish she would initiate more without having to play mind games. In other words, be blunt about it with your words and your touches. 'None of this soft kissing—be more aggressive.'" And when I asked men about what, if anything, they wanted to change with regard to initiation patterns in their relationship I heard things like "She could be more upfront about wanting sex" and "I want her to initiate . . . in a direct manner. Don't be subtle" and "I'd like her to initiate more frequently and more boldly." That word *boldly* , really catches me. Because while *women* might be thinking that they are being crystal clear that they are interested, he just might be missing it. Kevin spelled it out,

> "Sometimes she wants sex but also wants me to notice that she wants sex, so she wants me to make the first move, and I can be completely oblivious sometimes. This is frustrating. If she wants sex, why won't she just say so or do something about it! I'm right here!"

The other thing is that in a long-term partnership we interact with our partners so frequently that sometimes an action may be foreplay or initiation while other times it's a stand-alone activity. Take, for example, kissing, holding hands, or cuddling just to name a few. Sometimes we may kiss as a way to lead into sexual activity but other times we just want to make out. And we women might be *slightly* (OK, fine, *much* more) likely to tell our partner that our cuddling is "just cuddling, so you can forget whatever else you have in mind, buddy" but *less* likely to say, "Oh yeah, baby, this cuddle is a little more than a cuddle, wink wink." Sean told me of his confusion about not being sure sometimes whether his wife's cuddling or kissing was just that or if it was a form of foreplay:

> "I wish she would initiate more often and more assertively. I've gotten the 'snuggling/kissing isn't foreplay!' lecture enough times in my life—including from my wife—that I've trained myself to not think anything is being initiated until my genitals are being touched. So it's supremely frustrating when I'm told I missed out on an opportunity and the reason is along the lines of, 'Well, I was kissing you *that* way. Why didn't you take the hint?'"

While I'm not saying that blunt, here-I-am-let's-have-sex initiation isn't a huge aphrodisiac for men *sometimes*, leaning on it too often feeds into that stereotype that men will take any opportunity to have sex and that they don't need to feel romanced.

Well, you know by now where this is going, right?

WHERE IS THE LOVE?

The biggest misconception about men and sex that weaves its way throughout this book is that men's desire is surface level and that their desire is fairly easy to spark. And that just so happens to be a detail that also gets repeatedly overlooked when it comes to initiating sex with men. Women tend to think that when they *do* initiate, it can (or should) be simple and straightforward. They just present their naked selves or grab him randomly and it will do the trick. "You want sex, right? Here I am!" We *certainly* don't need to slowly seduce or romance him.

So one more time, louder for the folks in the cheap seats: Men. Want. To. Be. Romanced. Too.

Much more frequently than wanting to be "surprised" or "jumped," the thing that comes up in my research is that men don't *just* want their female partner to initiate sex; they want to be seduced by her. For example, listen to this description from Greg: "She tells me verbally when she is in the mood, but sometimes I would like her to 'act sexy' more often, for example, dressing in lingerie, dancing or moving sensually, etc."

I'll admit that when I was first processing men's descriptions of wanting their female partner to initiate sex, I thought it was mainly about her being seductive and sexy (like wearing lingerie), and I thought it might just feed into the myth that men are mostly turned on by physical cues. But as I continued in my research I realized that—*again*—this was a misperception I held about men and sex. As I heard from more and more men, I learned that these comments were less about what his partner was wearing or him wanting a stereotypical striptease or something more explicitly sexual. Rather, men were describing that they wanted their female partner to put in *effort*. They didn't want her to treat him like sex was a given, *just because he was a guy*.

For example, Kane described how his wife would often take this approach. She would undress in front of him but then expect that this action alone would get him turned on such that he would make the move on her:

> "She'll get naked and sort of expect me to initiate and lead the foreplay just because she's naked. But I still have to make the moves and work her up, and then she reacts with consent (or sometimes not if it turns out she's just not feeling it after all). But she doesn't actively try to see if I'm up for it, and I wish she would sometimes."

Dwayne similarly outlined how he would prefer his wife initiate sex with more effort, time, and build up. He said,

> "I would like her to do it more but also to do it more smoothly. She treats sex so robotically, in my opinion, and just sort of springs it on me without preamble or flirtation. Makes me feel a bit used."

Yes, he said *used*. As in, you just want to *use* me for sex. Which is clearly not framed as some kind of hot, kinky, or positive experience for him. And actually, on the far other end of the spectrum, sometimes men describe that wanting their female partner to initiate sometimes has almost nothing to do with *sex*. Rather they want their girlfriend to be the one to initiate *any* type of closeness and connection, like cuddling or romantic touching. Phillip described,

> "[I wish] she would initiate a deeper physical encounter more often. Hugging, kissing and holding hands it's about half and half. Cuddling and more I initiate substantially more often."

It's no coincidence that I've heard from many men that they want their female partner to initiate at times when they are feeling emotionally detached or insecure about themselves or their relationship. In that sense when women reach out for physical contact, they can help men feel cared for, seen, and loved. As Craig said, "I'd like her to be better at initiating sex, especially at times when I'm feeling emotionally distant." However, men often feel that their female partner doesn't know that this is an important part of his desire so they simply don't do it. As Alan described, "I would like my wife to initiate. Throughout our marriage I've felt as though she feels that men don't need to be romanced. We do."

WHY THIS MYTH IS A PROBLEM

As the saying goes, "We've always done it that way" is the most harmful sentence in the English language. And when it comes to the sexual initiation script between men and women I couldn't agree more. The reason that men traditionally initiate sex and women act as the gatekeepers stems from pretty outdated gendered "rules" that ultimately restrict how we express our sexuality.

Women: We have learned far too often, and for far too long, to be passive with our sexuality. To let men come to us. To wait for them to make the move first. And while in some ways that can feel nice (i.e., it makes us feel wanted, and to be fair, the person who says yes or no to sex *does* hold a certain level of control over the situation), it ultimately stifles our sexual agency.

By and large the women I meet who have concerns about a low libido will say that part of what continues to reinforce their concern is that they are consistently saying no to sex. They feel that their male partner is "always in the mood" and every time she says no it's another reminder that she doesn't want sex. But what if the tables were turned and *you* initiated sex (at least sometimes) and *he* said yes or no to your advances?

What if, instead of waiting for sex to be on *his* schedule, when *he's* in the mood, you made it happen when *you* were feeling horny or when *you* wanted to feel close? Paying attention to your sexual feelings and urges and acting upon them may just open up a world of possibilities in terms of better tuning into, and embracing, your sexuality.

Then if you are open to initiating sex, there is the whole *how* you're initiating piece, and what assumptions you're making about *his* sexuality in the process. Being clear and direct can absolutely work, but it's not necessarily a reflection of his desire being surface level and simplistic. It's also about him wanting to be *sure* you're in the mood and not misread your signs and risk rejection (which we'll get to next in the *rejection myth* discussion). Consider that he might not *always* be on the lookout for sex. That he wants to be *wanted* by you, *desired* by you, *needed* by you, and *loved* by you. And when you initiate sexual activity (or cuddling, kissing, or anything else in that realm) this functions as a little indicator that makes him think, "Oh good, she still wants me. She still loves me." Because, well, men are vulnerable, too, and these reassurances are hugely important to *all* of us.

Men: I'm a huge advocate for openly communicating your sexual wants and needs to your partner. So if you like when your wife or girlfriend initiates sex, find a way to share this with her. But the way you do this is important. Recognize that initiating sex is something she *may* feel uncomfortable or unfamiliar with or maybe just doesn't like doing. You need to share *your* personal reason of why you like her to initiate. If it makes you feel wanted, let her know that. If it helps relieve your worries of rejection, tell her that. And if you would be happy if she initiated even just cuddles on the couch, kissing before bed or hugs at random, make sure you've shared that with her too. As I mentioned in the chapter before, women's sexual initiation is a key part of men's desire to feel desirable. If this plays a factor for you, open up and let her in.

In addition, consider whether you're playing into a certain role yourself that's reinforcing this one-way initiation dynamic. If you're initiating even when you're not in the mood, stop. Maintenance sex is OK *sometimes*. Having sex when our partner wants it and we're only lukewarm is OK *sometimes*. But initiating sex you don't want because you feel you have to or that she would be disappointed if you didn't isn't helping anybody. And it's setting you up for bad sex. Plus, it's letting her off the hook for taking initiative and ownership of her sexuality and *you're* being negatively reinforced for having sex that you're only feeling "meh" about. And guess what—she can *feel* that on some level. And having sex to avoid a negative reaction (i.e., her disappointment) negatively impacts sexual satisfaction.

MYTH IN ACTION: COURTNEY AND DAVE

The Case of the Confused Mind Reader

Back to Courtney and Dave and a little background on how they first ended up in therapy. The couple had originally come, as most heterosexual couples do, to explore *her* low interest in sex. Dave described himself having a healthy sexual appetite but said Courtney would often turn him down. Courtney had a similar assessment of their situation. She said that Dave was *always* initiating sex and she was often the one saying no.

But as you may have guessed by now, there was a lot more happening under the surface. Because Courtney sometimes *did* feel interested in sex. Remember how she approached Dave on the couch that evening? Her actions were vague and her signs ultimately went unnoticed, but she *was* interested in sex and felt like she was making it known. So we picked up on what was going on for both of them that evening.

Dave started by explaining that he had no idea Courtney was trying to suggest sex. "She always tells me we don't cuddle enough. I thought this was one of those times she just wanted to be affectionate and *not* have me make it into something sexual. I never know what she wants. It's so confusing," he said, a bit defeated and frustrated.

We shifted to Courtney and *her* experience of that evening. Upon reflection she said she could understand how her intentions may not have been clear to Dave. However, that night she *wanted* him to take control of the situation. To her it felt like she was coming on strong, and when he didn't pick up on her mood she felt like she should give it a rest. She didn't want to put herself out there anymore. What she was doing already felt pretty big.

We dug a bit deeper into messages Courtney received about sex as a young woman growing up. She opened up about her older, sexually promiscuous sister who had gotten pregnant as a teenager. Courtney internalized her parents' disappointment and her sister's social isolation and attempted to balance her sister's behaviors by being the epitome of a proper, chaste young lady. Which meant repressing her sexual urges and certainly not acting on them. So putting herself out there, as she did with Dave that night on the couch, actually was a pretty big deal for her.

Armed with this new understanding of one another we embarked on a little experiment. What would happen if, instead of Dave initiating sex over the next two weeks, Courtney would first notice when she was in the mood and then she would try again to suggest it, but with a little more clarity from her and a little more curiosity and checking in from Dave. Courtney said she felt a little nervous about it. It was out of her comfort level. She worried it would feel forced. Awkward. Clunky. But with some gentle encouragement the couple agreed to give it a shot and see what happened. If it didn't work we agreed that we would try something different. No pressure.

When we met next time, they said Courtney had tried to initiate and it worked out better than expected. Well, to be fair, Courtney said it was "weird but good" and Dave said he really liked it. They told me about how when Courtney put her hand on Dave's leg one day, he checked in about what that action meant ("Are you . . . in the mood?"), and she gave him the nod that suggested it was more than a platonic touch. Dave felt less worried and more confident. Courtney said she liked it too. Instead of saying no to sex and feeling like the gatekeeper, *she* got to suggest sex. When *she* wanted it. When her sexual urge crept up, she thought, "OK, what do I want to do with this?" And she felt a bit of a thrill in sharing her desire with Dave. Which felt pretty good for a change.

SUMMARY

The myth that men *should* initiate (or like to initiate, or don't mind initiating) all sexual activity generally reinforces that sex-crazed male brain myth that we have worked so hard to debunk throughout this book.

- As teenagers, men and women receive very different messages about how to approach sexual activity.
- Boys learn push to the next level of sexual intimacy (i.e., initiate sex), whereas women learn to be skeptical of boys' advances and,

as a result, act as the gatekeepers who decide whether or not to let them in.

- This pattern continues to play out in romantic relationships. In fact, across studies *most* heterosexual couples report that men initiate the vast majority of sexual encounters.
- However, when asked how men feel about this pattern, most men indicate they would prefer that their female partner initiate sex more frequently.
- Bold sexual initiation helps men feel reassured that their female partner is interested and helps to reduce his fear of sexual rejection.
- Yet the piece that is most often ignored is men's need to be seduced, romanced, and cared about through women's sexual initiation.
- Taking a more active role in sexual initiation is something that may help women tap into their own sexual urges and take greater control over their sexuality and sexual urges.

MYTH 8

The Rejection Myth

"**H**e can't be serious," Maria thought to herself, again, as she pulled the bed covers more tightly around her. "*Really*. What is he *thinking*?"

It was "that time"—9 p.m. on Sunday night. Ross and Maria had been reading in bed to unwind before the workweek started back up. Like they always did. Then Maria noticed the familiar rustle beneath the sheets. It was this rustling that started off the usual chain reaction, beginning with Maria's resigned, deep sigh. Ross would dog-ear his book, slide his hand under the sheets, across the bed and start rubbing Maria's back.

"Here we go again," Maria would think. "Sunday night, as usual. Like clockwork. No romance, no build up. No spice, no excitement. Just like a well-oiled machine." Except that Maria didn't want to be part of that well-oiled machine anymore. In fact, she was getting more and more frustrated with the sex she and Ross were having. It was boring. It was predictable. And her frustration grew and grew until her anger started to bubble to the surface.

But what made this night different than most of the other Sundays at 9 p.m. was that instead of acquiescing and having missionary, fairly passionless sex, this time Maria snapped, "I can't do this anymore!!" she cried, in a way that was loud and abrasive for Maria but might have been just a harsh tone by anyone else's standards. "If we don't start having better sex I'm not sure this relationship is going to work!"

Ross lay there in shock. "What just happened? Did I do something wrong? I thought Maria liked having sex on Sundays. That's when we always do it. She said no to sex during the week already. And told me not to try to have sex right after dinner because she didn't like the smell of food on my breath. What's left? And aren't I the one putting in all the effort here? What is Maria upset for?"

Two weeks later Ross and Maria were sitting in my office describing this event.

* * *

Throughout this chapter I will outline how a pattern of sexual rejection that started *long before* this Sunday night set the stage for Maria and Ross to arrive at a place where neither was sexually satisfied.

This chapter will address how the couple came to participate in what I call the "sexual rejection dance." We will take a look at how young, single women learn to reject men's sexual advances during the courting and dating stage, and how those once adaptive responses stay with them and can negatively impact their intimate relationships later in life. We'll challenge those learned beliefs by examining research about how men *really* respond to their female partner's sexual rejection and how repeated rejection decreases men's sexual interest and leads to less effective initiations—ultimately resulting in less exciting sex for everyone involved.

THIS IS GOING TO HURT ME MORE THAN IT HURTS YOU

Before we talk about men and sexual rejection, let's first reflect on what rejection feels like for women. For some women, tapping into the experience of sexual rejection can be easy, while for others it can be a fairly difficult, even impossible, memory to conjure up (that is, some women may *never* have had an experience of sexual rejection). But when women *do* experience sexual rejection, most take it pretty hard.

In fact, I have worked with numerous heterosexual couples where the woman has stated, with a great deal of conviction, that she is no longer initiating sex because of "that time" (sometimes months, if not years earlier) when her partner turned down her sexual advances.

Can you imagine what would happen if men took that same approach? If men said that the *one time* they were turned down was so hurtful, so crushing, that they never put themselves back out there? That they never could bring themselves to initiate sex again? To risk that hurt? There would be *a lot* of celibate couples, I can tell you that much.

So why do we tend to think that rejection would hurt so much for women and not recognize that this hurt also exists for men?

It's probably safe to say that there aren't that many (if any) of us who believe the opposite of this myth to be true. That is, most people likely don't think, "Men love getting rejected!" But this myth isn't about liking or not liking to get rejected. It's about what rejection really *feels* like for men, and it's about *how* women reject sexual advances if they believe that their rejections have little to no impact on their male partner.

The reason a lot women don't think sexual rejection would (or should) hurt men is because of two main assumptions. The first assumption stems from the *selfish myth*, or the belief that men don't care about connecting and feeling close, they just want to "get off." It doesn't feel very romantic to think of our partner's sexual interest for us in this way. But if women believe this, of course they would be somewhat—or even *very*—dismissive of their partner's sexual advances. Hopefully it's clear by now, though, that men's motivations for sex are very removed from that limited idea. And that rather when men do reach out for sex, it's a bid for connection and closeness.

The second reason we might believe this rejection myth sounds something like: "Well, men initiate all the time, so it can't hurt that much because they must get used to it." The idea is that men initiate more sex so they should expect that many of those times, or at least some of those times, will result in rejection—so their hopes can only be so high to start with. But although the emotional hurt from rejection might not happen after the first rejection (although it can, and it does), after a few times this feeling of hurt absolutely resonates with men, too.

In fact, more and more often I hear men describe how much sexual rejection stings. That rejection makes them doubt their sexual abilities. That it makes them doubt their partner's feelings toward them. It makes them doubt their worth. It just plain makes them doubt and wonder, *is it me?*

In other words, just because sexual rejection might be more likely to occur to a man doesn't mean it's any easier to handle. In fact, it seems to be the opposite pattern. That is, the more often rejection happens, the more it can really hurt a man's confidence and self-esteem, and even decrease his own interest in sex.

THROWBACK TO YOUR BAR STAR DAYS

Before we go any further, I want to address that there are very good reasons that women have come to learn that their sexual rejections don't really hurt men (or why some women have maybe never even considered the impact of their rejections). And it goes back to their single, dating days.

Most women reading this can remember some version of *that* creep at the club. You're dancing to some pulsating drum and bass. You're having fun when a guy comes up and starts dancing with you. He seems cute. You feel might even feel flattered that he has approached you. But then he starts putting his hands all over you and getting way too close. He clearly wants something more and isn't reading the signs that you *just* want to dance. You get frustrated, push his hands away and tell him to get lost. You're just here to have fun with your friends.

Or perhaps you're at the bar, getting a drink, and find out your drink has been paid for by the guy at the other end. You say thanks and start chatting until he enters into "So, what do I get in return?" territory. You roll your eyes, put the drink down, tell him to "have a nice life," and go back to find your friends.

Sound familiar? Whether or not you frequented the bar or experienced these specific situations, you've likely had some version of "that guy" you don't know all that well approach you, only to find out his main focus was sex. You don't feel great about it because, well, *you're a person and being reduced to a sexual object is offensive to say the very least!* and you tell him off accordingly. So you put him in the category of "creep" and are very unlikely to consider what impact your rejection had on him. What could he have lost out on anyway? Another "notch on his belt?" Nothing for you to worry about, that's for sure.

And in these situations that reaction makes complete sense. Particularly because a man you don't know is not being respectful of your boundaries and is making assumptions that he should have some sort of access to your body.

EVEN BAR STARS HURT SOMETIMES

OK, let's take a tiny leap forward in the dating and relationship timeline. We aren't quite at the relationship phase yet; we're just courting. Maybe we're open to a flirtatious interaction to suss out whether we want things to move forward.

So this time, imagine you're in a lounge. The music sounds good; you can sip your drink without someone bumping and spilling it on you, and you can actually talk to your friends. Then you happen to notice an attractive guy across the room. You catch each other's eyes a few times. He comes over and asks if he can buy you a drink. This isn't one of the "creeps" we talked about before. He seems like a perfectly nice, normal guy and you're interested in chatting with him. So you agree. You flirt a bit, you talk, you laugh. Then he invites you to his apartment for a nightcap. You decide to go home with him and start making out. Then you catch yourself. You realize it might not be a good idea for you to stay any longer and ask him to call a taxi for you to get home. Let's just end things here, thanks very much.

How do you imagine that would feel? Do you think he would be disappointed? Embarrassed? Angry? Relieved?

Dutch researchers Hanneke de Graaf and Theo Sandfort conducted a study exploring exactly this question.[1] Specifically, the researchers asked young men and women (aged eighteen to thirty) to read hypothetical scenarios (similar to the scenario you just read) in which they were to imagine meeting someone they were attracted to at the bar, followed by being sexually rejected by that person. After they read the scenario they were asked how likely they might be to experience various emotions.

After reading and imaging this scenario, the researchers asked the participants to rate the degree to which they might experience thirty-two various emotions on a scale of 1–5 (1 being "not at all applicable" and 5 being "very much applicable"). They asked about some *positive* emotions that may or may not follow rejection such as *relief, happiness*, and *enjoyment* as well as some negative emotions such as *disappointment, embarrassment, anger*, and *inferiority*. The researchers were also interested in whether there were any gender differences with regard to emotional reactions to sexual rejection. And they concluded that men were *less likely* to harbor negative emotions when they imagined being rejected than were women.

But how much less likely?

The differences were statistically significant (i.e., the differences were determined to be related to something other than chance alone), but the actual differences, or what we researchers call "meaningful significance," were somewhat small. Specifically, on a scale of 1–5, women reported they would experience an average negative emotional reaction of 2.83 while men reported an average negative emotional reaction of 2.17.

Another way of interpreting the findings is that *both men and women were somewhat hurt by imagining their sexual advances were rejected.* After all, there is no finite amount of "hurt from rejection" that people can experience. Just because women reported slightly more negative emotional reactions to (hypothetical) sexual rejection, doesn't mean men didn't, and don't, experience *any* negative emotional reactions. But we don't tend to think of differences this way. As we explored in The Gender Myth chapter, we have a habit of focusing and exaggerating any and all differences before we consider shared experiences.

And there is more. Even with these relatively small gender differences, the authors stated that men might have been less likely than women to *admit* they experienced negative emotions following rejection. In their own words, "It could, however, also be that men are less willing to admit that they are hurt. After all, men's gender script prescribes them not to express their emotions or vulnerability."[2] In other words, men might not feel comfortable discussing the impact of sexual rejection or admit that it hurts because it could be perceived as "unmanly" to do so. (I'm going to ask you to hold on to the word *vulnerability*, because I'll come back to it in a few pages.)

At this point you might be thinking, "But wait! That study focused on casual sex, with someone the participants didn't know and may never see again. And it was hypothetical. The study findings don't give a sense of how men experience rejection in *real life*, with a *real* partner. A partner they have *real* feelings for. What does rejection look like for men in the context of a committed longer-term relationship? What does rejection feel like for my husband or boyfriend?"

I'm glad you asked.

WHAT'S LOVE GOT TO DO WITH IT?

During my research I interviewed men in long-term relationships about whether there were times where they felt less desire, or maybe even experienced no sexual desire at all. Which isn't a question that gets asked to men that often. After all, the assumption is that they feel desire all the time so how could there be examples of *not* feeling desire? And quite honestly, I wasn't sure how men were going to respond to this question. Would they laugh? Brush me off? Continue to play into the stereotype and not admit to anything other than high and constant interest in sex?

Well, as you likely know by now, no—not even close.

But even though I had a hypothesis that men might experience decreased or no sexual desire at some points in their lives and their relationships, I didn't know what might be responsible for that lack of interest. It surprised me when the *most frequently* described situation when their sexual desire decreased—a situation mentioned by almost every man I interviewed—was when their female partner rejected their sexual advances.[3]

For example, look at this quote from one participant I talked with, Kyle, who discussed the impact sexual rejection had on him:

> "If she doesn't want me, she somehow is not interested in me . . . it offends me somewhere inside. I don't feel this, extremely being offended, being traumatized, but maybe somehow subconsciously that's how it happens . . . I know she is not interested in me and she doesn't like me. Doesn't want me. It's like forget it. I don't feel it anymore."

The thing that I find so profound about Kyle's words is that he is not only talking about disappointment from sexual rejection in the sense of missing out on a sexual encounter. He describes being hurt and offended. Kyle isn't saying, she doesn't want sex *right now*. The feeling is that through sexual rejection it's an indication that she doesn't want *me*.

But most women don't think about men's reactions to their sexual rejections looking or feeling like that. It's not uncommon for women to think that when they reject that their partner, he just missed out on having sex that night. Or women are so frustrated that their partner chose the wrong time to initiate that they don't even care how he feels after the rejection. Because he *must* have seen it coming, right? It's as if women have been cued to go right back to the bar "creep" version of men.

Most of the men I talked with weren't just talking about rejection here and there that could be chalked up to bad timing; for example, he's in "the mood" but she has a legitimate headache, is sick, is in a bad mood, and so on. That's going to happen. It does happen. In every relationship. Because the idea that we would feel sexual interest at the exact same time as our partner every time over multiple years is a nice but pretty far-fetched idea. There are going to be plenty of times where either partner says, "No, not tonight honey."

But some men I interviewed talked about the impact of *regular* rejection of their sexual advances that wore them down over time. Regular rejection that made them question themselves, their relationship, and ultimately negatively impacted their self-esteem. Men even indicated that having their sexual advances rejected over and over actually decreased their own level of interest in sex, something that appeared to be an adaptive, protective strategy.

Here are quotes from a few more men I talked with describing the impact that regular rejection of their sexual advances had on their own interest in sex:

> "It is frustrating, it's upsetting, annoying at times. [Sex] has been so less frequent lately that it gets frustrating. And eventually it makes you not want to try anymore, or less frequently. That's what is ending up happening. She's not as interested in it anymore and it's making me feel that way too."

> "When you're the guy and you're always the one to make the moves all the time, and your partner's always the one saying "no, no, no, no" you start getting very aware . . . depressed, and wondering whether or not something is going on. Whether or not it's you."

> "I'm usually a very positive person, but when it comes to sex, it's tough to stay positive or imagine [sex] when you're always getting rejected. So it's easier not to think about it."

These responses represent the sentiments I've heard from more and more men during research and in therapy. Sexual rejection hurts. And men take sexual rejection personally. It can make men doubt themselves and their relationships to the point that they pull back and sometimes shut down, emotionally and sexually.

PUBLIC SPEAKING, ASKING FOR A RAISE, AND . . . INITIATING SEX?

So it's clear that sexual rejection doesn't feel good. *For women or for men.* Which brings us to some important questions: Why does rejection hurt so much? Why would it take such a toll on men's self-esteem? And why would men so actively work to avoid experiencing it again?

Those might seem like silly questions with obvious answers. I mean, who *wants* to be rejected? Clearly rejection is an unpleasant and unwanted feeling. However, this myth stems from another myth we have addressed already in this book: the *selfish myth* (or the assumption that men only want sex for their own pleasure, not connection). The thought connecting the *selfish* and *rejection myths* is that if men initiate sex and their efforts are rejected, it can't hurt that much because all they lost out on was the physical act of sex or "getting off."

I hope by this point in the book I've been able to debunk the idea that all men want from sex is sexual gratification. If, instead, we can acknowledge that sex is a way for men to feel close and connected to their partner, to be accepted, to show love, and to feel love, then it makes sense that it would be a pretty vulnerable thing to continue putting themselves out there again and again, especially if they thought there was a good chance of being turned down. (This is where I revisit that word I mentioned before: *vulnerability*.)

Dr. Brené Brown, if you're not familiar with her work, is a vulnerability expert and a bit of a TED Talk sensation.[4] (She has also written some really excellent books that are referenced at the end of this book if you're interested in reading more about vulnerability, shame, and courage.)[5] Dr. Brown acknowledges that a lot of men and women, young and old, struggle with the word *vulnerability* because it *sounds* weak. When we hear *vulnerable* we think *defenseless*, *exposed*, and *susceptible*. And for many people the thought of being vulnerable brings about a quick reaction along the lines of "No thank you!"

But how does Dr. Brown define this scary-sounding word? She defines vulnerability as "uncertainty, risk and emotional exposure."[6] And Brown very clearly describes vulnerability as a strength, *not a weakness*. Because it's not very comfortable to expose ourselves emotionally without knowing whether the person we are being vulnerable with will accept and respond to us in the way we need. And for many of us (or maybe even all of us, at least sometimes) it's easier to avoid that vulnerability by *not* putting ourselves out there. It's sometimes easier to pretend that our partner didn't hurt us. Or that our partner *isn't capable* of having such a strong impact on us. But when we numb and avoid being vulnerable, we also lose out on the chance to be our authentic selves and experience the ultimate close connection with our partner, because we are always holding something back.

Interestingly, in her book *Daring Greatly* Brené Brown even lists sexual initiation as a vulnerable activity for men (and women), but something that often gets overlooked.[7] Now, quite frankly, I have yet to hear any man spontaneously use the word *vulnerability* with regard to his sexuality. But since conducting my research I've framed sexual rejection with men this way during therapy to see how the word fits for size. I describe how when we initiate sex we are putting ourselves out there without certainty of what our partner's response will be. There is an inherent element of risk with that. How much do I want (or even need) to feel close right now? How badly do I want to be held? Will they or won't they say yes? And am I willing to find out?

And more often than not, after I describe sexual initiation and rejection in this way, the man in front of me and his female partner tend to take a deep breath and sigh. It hits home. Because if that's not emotional exposure, I don't know what is.

FACT: MEN AVOID SEX TO AVOID SEXUAL REJECTION

At this point you might be thinking, "OK, men experience more hurt from sexual rejections than we typically acknowledge. That's helpful to know."

But there's more.

The next phase of the sexual rejection dance is how men adjust their behaviors and actions in sexual relationships as a result of repeated rejection, and how that impacts the *way* they initiate and whether they even notice their partner's sexual openness or sexual cues in the first place.

Do you remember Dr. Muise's study from The Gender Myth chapter? The one that asked how good men and women were at perceiving their partner's interest in sex? The one that found that men missed many of the signs that their female partner was feeling sexual desire, thereby believing her interest in sex was lower than it actually was? Well, another important finding emerged from that study that has to do with rejection.

A quick reminder: The study was a three-part analysis. In parts 1 and 2, the authors (after analyzing the combined data of 128 couples) found that across both studies there was a similar pattern of men *underperceiving* their female partner's interest in sex. So Muise and colleagues conducted a third study to explore *why* this might be the case. And they just happened to focus on the potential role of rejection.

The third of Muise's studies included 101 (mostly) heterosexual couples between the ages of eighteen and fifty-three, in relationships that ranged from six months to twenty-two years.[8] Over the course of three weeks the couples were asked to keep a daily diary of their sexual activity as well as their level of sexual desire and their relationship satisfaction. The researchers also happened to ask about the potential motivation to avoid rejection. It was measured with the following straightforward question: "I did not want my partner to reject me" (with responses ranging from 1 indicting "not at all important" to 7 indicating "extremely important").

The researchers concluded that on days when men were *particularly motivated to avoid rejection*, they were more likely to *underperceive* their partner's interest in sex. In other words, when men reported feeling that the possibility of being rejected was just too much (for whatever reason, or reasons, that might be—say, feeling insecure, having a bad day, previously receiving some less than stellar feedback from a boss), they missed the sexual cues from their partner. They did not initiate sex. They were less likely to even report *thinking* about sex.

This appears to be an adaptive response, when a guy might consider, "Hey, maybe my partner isn't in the mood and it would be too risky today to get it wrong. Too risky to think they did have an interest and then experience rejection again. Maybe I'll just leave it alone and see if there is anything good to watch on Netflix . . ."

Although that's not the story we usually hear about men, is it?

FROM SEXUAL STUD TO AWKWARD LOVER

So far we have discussed a number of components of the sexual rejection dance:

1. Women have learned to detect and reject sexual advances from random men who just want sex. And these learned responses can show up in their intimate relationships when women get the sense that their male partner *just* wants sexual gratification.
2. However, sexual rejection is an emotionally hurtful experience for men because in intimate relationships, it is a way for men to express their feelings and feel closer to their partner.
3. The more often sexual rejection happens to men, the more (*not less*) it can hurt.
4. Because initiating sex is a vulnerable situation, when faced with the possibility of sexual rejection, men experience less sexual desire themselves, and they avoid initiating sex to avoid experiencing more rejection.

So *how* exactly do men initiate sex when they are worried about the potential experience of sexual rejection? Well it appears that regular rejection tends to result in men using *less effective initiation strategies* to avoid sticking their neck out and getting hurt.

Specifically, at the earlier stages of a relationship many men describe being more likely to put a fair bit of effort into setting the mood before sex. They might have engaged in more or longer foreplay, lit candles, or whispered sweet nothings in their partner's ear. But over time, if they are rejected more and more regularly, it becomes increasingly risky to keep putting in that same level of effort. So instead of jumping in with both feet they may test the temperature in less sexy ways. Say, by giving a nudge at a seemingly inopportune time (like, say, right as you're about sit down with your favorite book) or perhaps bluntly saying, "So . . . wanna do it?"

It makes sense though, doesn't it? If we keep reaching out to someone over and over again and they keep saying no, over time we tend to get the idea that we should give it a rest. It's what makes us adaptive and effective social creatures. We take social cues, learn from them, and adjust our behavior accordingly.

It's like those friends we keep inviting out for drinks who always have an excuse why they can't make it. Maybe it was fine or understandable the first time. Or even a couple of times. But once there is a pattern established, you might shift from inviting them out every time to making plans with other friends and inviting them to join last minute to, well, maybe just not inviting them out at all anymore.

Not only does sexual initiation after repeated rejection not feel great for men, but women sometimes share that their male partners' initiation just isn't doing the trick for them either. It's too subtle. Or, alternatively, too bold and obvious.

So, is it possible that type of awkward initiation is related to sexual rejection? I say, *yes, absolutely.*

In addition to interviewing men about their sexual desire, I have also interviewed women about their sexual experiences in the context of long-er-term relationships. In one study, I recruited two groups of young, adult women who self-selected into one of two groups.[9] The first was a group of women who self-identified as having high desire at the beginning of their longer-term relationship, followed by a drop in desire over time. The other was a group of women who felt that the passion they felt in the early stages of their relationship was still alive and well years later. Then we compared the two groups to see if there were any differences that might explain why some women would continue to feel high desire over time while others might experience a decrease.

It turned out that some women who self-identified as having a de-crease in their sexual desire over the course of their relationship indicated that they could become easily turned off when their male partner initiated sex in one of two ways: *too subtly* or *too boldly*. Both were described as ineffective and frustrating. On the other hand, the women in the high desire group did not describe this concern.

Take a look at how a couple of these women describe the perceived ineffective ways their partners are initiating sex in their own words: "Sometimes he'll say 'Hey—want to have sex?' and I'm like 'No.' Too strong. Too blunt." Or "He'll roll over and start rubbing my back while I'm about to fall asleep and I'm like . . . are you kidding me right now?"

Now it's possible that these specific male partners were a bit clueless or ineffective when it came to sexual initiation with these women. Or that these female participants were particular about what they wanted from their male partners, making it difficult for them to do anything "right." But my colleagues and I made another hypothesis: perhaps the women who had lower desire and described saying no to sex more regularly had partners who were nervous or uncomfortable putting themselves out there as much as they used to earlier on in the relationship. And because women in our study indicated that their desire was higher at the beginning of their relationships, perhaps initiation patterns changed over time, which might be partially responsible for the cycle of lower desire and passion.

We now know from the research presented earlier in this chapter that this very well could be the case with these women. It's also *most certainly* the case with many couples I talk with in therapy.

SEX IS LIKE ANGEL-FOOD CAKE

The impact of the *rejection myth*, like all myths addressed in this book, exists because of an interaction between men and women. And the myth can only be broken if both men and their female partners work together to take ownership for their role in contributing to and reinforcing it. I've been talking a lot about men's experiences, but I'm going to switch to discussing the impact of *how* women reject their male partner's sexual advances.

Before I expand I want to make one thing absolutely clear: no person (man or woman) should ever have sex when it's truly unwanted. In the world of rape culture we live in, it's particularly important to explicitly state: we are *always* allowed to say we're not in the mood, and we should always have that need respected.

However, it is important for women to consider the impact that our sexual rejections have on the men we love and are in a healthy, safe relationship with.

Some of the women I work with in therapy admit to feeling their partner's interest in sex and their initiation of sexual activity can feel annoying. It can feel like pestering. And they just want to make it stop. So they say no, with some level of contempt. They pull away quickly. They roll their eyes and say, "Are you kidding me? You know I have to get up early tomorrow." And, from what I see, it's the regular rejection, over and over again, and *the way* that rejection is conveyed that have the biggest impact on men.

Let me explain it with cake. Say you go out to a dinner party and the host offers you a slice of cake for dessert. And say that night you're full and don't have much of a sweet tooth. So you say no thank you and move on. Not a big deal. Right?

But what if you found out that the person who made the cake made it especially for you. They remember you saying you used to love angel food cake as a kid. They handpicked the strawberries from their backyard garden. And it took them hours to bake and prepare. Then would you say no? I would suggest that at minimum, if you were still really not in the mood for cake (which, again, is allowed), you would let them down very, very easily. Or perhaps, take a few moments to digest and consider having a piece of cake later in the evening. Or take a slice of cake home with you to eat later.

If you're still with me and haven't run to the kitchen to satisfy your sweet tooth, let's take that same dynamic and apply it to sex and rejection. From my experience, women who say no to their partner's sexual advances think that he just picked up a cheap cake from the grocery store and it's not a big deal to say no. But in actuality, the offer might be more akin to the homemade angel food cake I just described.

And don't you *want to know* if your partner baked you a homemade cake?

WHY THIS MYTH IS A PROBLEM

You might be thinking, "OK I'm pretty sure we're doing the sexual rejection dance. Now what?" As with every myth addressed in this book, breaking old assumptions and behavior patterns requires changes by *both* partners.

Women: Rejection of sexual advances in an intimate relationship is inevitable. It's not about *if* you reject (everyone does and that's perfectly acceptable); it's about *how* you reject and what assumptions you might be making when you do.

Pay close attention the next time your boyfriend or husband initiates sex and you're not in the mood. How did you say no? Was it through body language (like rolling over quickly or forcefully pulling your arm away?), or was it verbal rejection (like "Sigh . . . no not now" or "Ugh. Not happening, buddy"). Try noticing if there is a pattern emerging. Ask yourself, am I always (or often) rejecting like this?

Then take it a step further and ask yourself, what assumptions am I making about his interest in sex when I'm saying no? Am I assuming he only wants sexual gratification? Or that he wants a chance to feel close and connected to me? Am I frustrated that he wants sex *again*? Or am I considering the vulnerability involved in putting himself out there even though he knows that he might get hurt again?

Next, consider if there are other ways you can respond to his sexual initiations. Perhaps you'll be more open to sex if you adjust your assumptions and see his initiation as a bid for closeness or connection instead of sexual gratification. However, if sex is unwanted (or you're simply not in the mood, or the timing isn't great)—you're *always* allowed to say no. If you are just not in the mood, there are plenty of ways to let him down gently. In fact, as part of my most recent research study I asked men about how they prefer to be rejected if their female partner just isn't in the mood. One of the main themes that emerged was that if you say no, it helps if you provide a follow-up option for another time. For example, "Tonight I really just want to go to bed, but can we set aside some time this weekend to have sex?" That way it's not a big daunting no; it's a *softer* no with an implied follow-up yes at a later date.

Another thing men shared is that rejection is harder when *all* physical touch is taken off the table. As I mentioned earlier, sometimes men are reaching out for connection and closeness when they initiate sex. Sometimes they just want to feel loved. So, if you don't want sex, that's fine, but they may be more hurt if you pull away from them all together. If you would be open to cuddling, say that! One participant said it's helpful "if she doesn't cease physical contact all together, and we can continue to be in [physical] contact." That might look something like "It's been a long day and sex is the last thing on my mind. Can I unwind for a few minutes and then we sit and cuddle on the couch instead?"

Men: I don't need to tell you this, but sexual rejection is inevitable. You're never going to bat a thousand. The biggest thing you can do is risk being vulnerable and share with your partner what you really get from having sex with her. If you act like all you want from sex is a physical release, your partner will, understandably, believe that's all that matters and treat your sexual initiation accordingly. Of course sex feels good (at least it should). But if you *also* like sex because it allows you to feel close to your partner or if you like sex because it validates your feelings for one another, *tell her*. It's brave and courageous to share your emotions and feelings. And women want to hear it. Take the risk.

The other important component here is to reach out for emotional connection and closeness in other ways than just through sex. If you truly want to feel close and connected, consider how holding hands, cuddling, or kissing more (without it necessarily leading to sexual activity) might satisfy those needs between sexual encounters. This also can help reassure your partner that you want her, and that sex is just one avenue of achieving this. Take it one step further? If what you're really craving is physical touch, tell her you would be happy cuddling if she isn't in the mood for sex.

Finally, consider the ways that you *personally* find rejection to be a bit more manageable (versus when it's particularly hurtful). Throughout my research men have, *on average*, preferred to be let down with an honest reason, while still maintaining some physical connection and with a suggestion of a future time for sex. However, there were also men who said they prefer a white lie over the truth. In other words, there isn't one size fits all when it comes to rejection. Think about your personality and your relationship and let your partner know what helps and what hurts. Chances are, she'll do her best to accommodate your needs as best as possible when she isn't in the mood.

MYTH IN ACTION: ROSS AND MARIA

The Case of the Sexual Rejection Dance

As I mentioned at the beginning of the chapter, Ross and Maria's sex life looked something like this: Ross would initiate sex, often on Sunday nights. Ross said he was no longer experiencing much sexual desire himself, so when he did initiate sex it was pretty basic. A tap on the shoulder or rub on the back while Maria was reading in bed. Something Maria said "bored her" and something Ross said felt awkward but at least he could say he was trying. Maria would sometimes roll her eyes and he would back down. If they did have sex it was missionary. Ross would often climax but said he could take the sex or leave it. Maria said she just closed her eyes and waited for it to be over.

One day, after a few sessions working together, Maria suddenly blurted something out. She said that she did in fact have an interest in sex. And she yearned for more sexual excitement and variety. And she worried that Ross didn't have it in him to fulfill those needs. She thought

Ross was only a Sunday night, missionary-style kind of guy and she couldn't take that boredom anymore.

"Wow," I thought to myself. How long had Maria been feeling her desire had been stifled? What did she actually want from their sexual relationship? How did Ross feel hearing Maria say that she wanted more sexually and he might not be able to fulfill those needs? And how did the couple get to this breaking point where a *humdrum* sex life was actually loaded with so many other feelings?

Well, as we explored this pattern Ross explained that he had shut down. Emotionally and sexually. He admitted that, although he used to have a higher interest in sex, he felt that over and over again he just wasn't "doing it right" for Maria. He would try touching her shoulder, her hips, her butt, and it wouldn't work. He would try to be flirtatious at dinner, out with friends, alone while watching TV on the couch, and it was always the "wrong time." And the kicker was that Maria wasn't telling him what she wanted or what might work better. More and more often Ross said he felt that he was being criticized and his efforts weren't worth it. So to save face he would tap Maria on her shoulder, cringe internally waiting for her response, and then either roll back over and read or have pretty passionless sex.

We had to make a game plan. How could both Ross and Maria work together to change this pattern?

First, we validated Ross's bravery for sharing the impact that rejection was having on him. Because without that crucial piece, the next bit of our work may have never happened. And even though he feared Maria would think less of him (he said he worried she wouldn't see him as "a man" anymore), Maria cried and said she appreciated his honesty so much more and thought he was strong to share his fears with her. In other words, she wanted to be let in. She could feel him shut down and was desperate to know more. The vulnerability was actually seen by Maria as a strength.

As we moved forward Maria agreed to be more cognizant of Ross's advances and the impact her rejections had on him. She took his experience of sex and rejection to heart. She realized she was wanted and that Ross wanted more. On one hand she said it made her sad, to know he was struggling. And on the other hand she felt good—knowing he cared so much. And not just about sex. About her. And about the future of their relationship. This actually made her open up more to sexual encounters. She found herself saying yes more often. Because she *also* wanted to feel close to Ross and now saw sex as a way to do that (and not just a way to experience pleasurable sensations). She also paid more attention to how she said no when she really wasn't in the mood and promised she wouldn't sit and stew until her frustrations bubbled over again.

Ross agreed that if Maria could tell him a bit more about what she liked, when she was in the mood, and what felt good (i.e., give positive reinforcement instead of just no's and criticism) he would try to be brave and work through the past hurt to initiate again in a more bold and sexy way—and not always on Sundays.

SUMMARY

Assumptions about how men experience sexual rejection result in a sexual rejection dance that makes sex less satisfying for both men and women.

- Women have learned to be wary of men's sexual advances. Although this was adaptive and helpful at one point, continuing to hold on to assumptions about men "only wanting one thing" can be damaging once we enter committed long-term relationships.
- Sexual rejection is hard for both women and men. In fact, both genders report experiencing some negative emotions, even when imagining being rejected in a hypothetical casual sexual encounter.
- Men who experience constant, regular rejection from their female partners report it having a negative impact on their self-esteem and their own interest in sex.
- In fact, research shows that men are motivated to *avoid* rejection in their intimate relationships and that this avoidance adjusts their sexual behaviors.
- Specifically, men who experience regular rejection often avoid initiating and therefore experience decreased sexual desire.
- Women whose partners initiate in less vulnerable ways describe feeling sexually frustrated by ineffective initiation that is too blunt or too subtle.
- By observing *how* women say no to—and questioning assumptions about *why* men are initiating—sex, heterosexual couples can reset the negative pattern that contributes to frustrating sexual encounters (or non-encounters) and ultimately feel closer to our partners.

MYTH 9

The Opportunity Myth

"Don't make me remind you why *I* don't initiate sex anymore," Cheryl said to Jason, with the slightest touch of contempt.

Had the couple been at home, Jason might have left the room in a huff. But here they were, sitting in my office. And as their therapist, I was most certainly going to follow up on that comment.

I thought to myself, "You *never* initiate?" I ask: "What happened?"

Cheryl described how it all stemmed back to a situation early on in their marriage—*fifteen* years ago. She said the couple had hit their first sexual slump. They went a couple of weeks without sex. It felt weird when up until that point they had been having sex every time they saw each other. But then they got married and moved in together and they just seemed to have lost their mojo. Cheryl said she wanted to do something fun to spice things up. So she bought a red lace teddy to surprise Jason.

"That's great," I thought to myself. "She's asserting her sexual agency and initiating sex. Gold star."

The problem? Jason didn't respond the way Cheryl had anticipated. Instead of salivating at the mouth and jumping her right then and there, he turned her down. They didn't have sex. Cheryl ended up crying in the bathroom and stuffing her lace teddy in the bottom drawer of her armoire, never to be seen again.

That was Cheryl's memory of the event. She said it was the most embarrassing thing that's ever happened to her.

Jason, on the other hand, said he barely remembers that night. He looks baffled and says it seems "weird" that he would have said no in a situation like that. He would *love* it if she would wear something sexy like that for him now.

"Fat chance," Cheryl replies.

* * *

This chapter addresses a myth that stems from the belief that men *always* want sex. That is, if we believe men's desire really is (or should be) *that* high and constant, then when *women* initiate sex, obviously he should drop everything he's doing and say yes. With enthusiasm. And gratitude. After all, he's getting what *he* wants. Right?

Well . . . maybe not.

There are plenty of times when men may say no to sex, and even more times where men *want* to say no to sex but feel they *should* say yes because this is what is expected of them. Over the course of this chapter we will focus on the pressure men can face to say yes to all sexual opportunities that come their way, what happens when men say yes to sex (when they would *prefer* to say no), and what can happen for women when their partner says no when they were hoping for a yes (hint: we tend to take it very personally, but I'm here to suggest we probably shouldn't).

NEVER HAVE I EVER

"If it's there, you'll probably take it."

"I've never not wanted sex when it's on offer."

"No . . . I have a high libido and like having sex at the drop of a hat."

These are just some of the responses I've received when I asked men in my research, "Can you remember a time where you weren't in the mood for sex? Or when you might have turned an opportunity for sex down?"

So, if you're thinking that men tend to take any sexual opportunity that comes their way—you're in good company. Because even some men I've spoken with are inclined to agree that they wouldn't turn down sex if the opportunity was presented to them. Sometimes they simply cannot recall a time they said no to sex. It's as if the first thing that comes to mind seems to be "I love sex—why would I say no? That doesn't sound like me!"

Another participant I interviewed said it was not in men's "nature" to turn down a sexual opportunity:

> "I think it's how guys are built. Their metabolism or whatever. . . . Guys will not say no as often as the ladies will. . . . More of a guy thing, no matter what we'll say yes. . . . A guy will more like, in general again, will not say no. It's not in their habit, their nature."

And I'll admit, if these descriptions truly and fully encapsulated men's experiences of sexual desire, then *of course* women would be devastatingly insulted if their partner said no to sex. After all, these men are saying they *never* turn down sex. So then if they did say no, well then, *yeah*, their partners would be spinning their heads trying to figure out what is wrong. *Is it him?* Or, perhaps even worse, *Is it me?*

But, if the conversations I had with men stopped there, I wouldn't be writing this book. The reason I *am* writing this book is because these conversations almost without exception go somewhere deeper.

BUT FIRST, WINE

"Can I get you anything? A cup of tea? Or . . . maybe a glass of wine?" My friend asks one night, a bit coyly.

"Oh, you know my policy! I never turn down a glass of wine!" I say with a grin.

It's a little joke my girlfriend and I have. She knows my answer before she even asks the question. Because we *love* wine. We aren't what you would call wine connoisseurs, but we know what we like. Red over white. Cab sauv over pinot noir. Bonus points if there is a cute or quirky label. (Yeah, we are *those* wine drinkers.)

And what could be better than saying yes to *something* you love *with* someone you love?

But occasionally, just *occasionally*, I'll say no to the offer. I'm driving. Or I'm feeling under the weather and tea would be a better call.

And then there are times where I *think* about saying no, and some part of me *wants* to say no. Perhaps I started going to the gym again and am trying to make healthier choices. Or I want to feel 100 percent in the morning so I can be super productive. Or maybe I overindulged on the weekend and I think my body would benefit from some water. But I can still find myself inclined to say, "Sure, bend my rubber arm!" Because that's what I do. I say *yes* to a glass of wine because I love it and, well, like I said, it's my policy.

But whether or not wine is your vice—or if it's beer, chips, or cheese—do you know that feeling I'm talking about? Where you surprised yourself by saying no to something you really like? Or you *thought* about saying no to something you really like but you said yes because (a) you love that thing so much that, of course, you *should* want it, and (b) you wonder if your friend who offered you wine (or beer, chips, cheese) really wanted some too and might be disappointed if you didn't join in?

This simile is only going to hold for so long so I'll pause there and say this: the research shows that sometimes men feel the same way when it comes to sex.

SICK AND TIRED

First things first. There is one particularly big reason that men report saying no to sex—the type of no that would be akin to saying no to a glass of wine because you're driving. In other words, a reason that just makes so much sense *even* if you're thinking that men are always inclined to say yes to sex. Specifically, if I ask men whether they have ever said no to sex, they may *start* by saying no, but then follow it up with "Oh, well unless I'm sick that is."

Actually, some men I've spoken with used feeling ill as the most likely reason they would not be in the mood for sexual activity. One man I spoke with described rarely being uninterested in sex, suggesting that serious illness would be the only factor to reduce his desire. He said, "The only time that would happen would be if you're in a place where you're extremely ill or bed-ridden." Other men I've talked to found it difficult to fathom the idea of not having desire or saying no to a sexual encounter. In that sense, not being in the mood for sex was described as an almost hypothetical situation; as Nate described, "I suppose, I guess . . . if there was a time I was sick for a long period of time?"

Similarly, having a chronic medical illness is also a reason some men report turning down a sexual opportunity. For example, when I spoke with Darryl, who had a history of chronic back pain, if he would ever say no to sexual advances from his wife, he responded, "I very rarely say no. And if I do, it's usually because I have a headache or am in a lot of pain."

And the thing is, when men are sick, most women probably aren't even feeling all hot and bothered to have sex with them anyway! Maybe they've been wearing the same pajama pants for three days straight, have Kleenex strewn around them, and could use a shower. So the chances of women wanting sex with their boyfriends or husbands during those time periods are probably slim to none. Sex doesn't even spring to mind. Or, if it did, it would be pretty easy to accept they weren't in the mood. At least it's definitively not personal. But what about when men aren't in the mood and they aren't sick? When men are just feeling, well, *tired*?

SURE SEX IS COOL, BUT HAVE YOU EVER HAD EIGHT HOURS OF SLEEP?

It's been a long day. You want to get close to your partner. It's been a while since you had sex. The kids are finally sleeping and the house is quiet. And clean. And *finally* you have a moment to yourselves where there is nothing that needs to get done. You think it might be a good opportunity to have sex. So you lean over toward your partner in bed and give them a kiss. But they don't return it with much enthusiasm. They say, "I'm tired. Can we try another time?"

How do you react? Are you taken aback? Frustrated? Annoyed? Understanding? Flabbergasted?

Well, it might depend on the circumstances, but when women are feeling like *they* have enough energy to have sex, they tend to be a little bit hurt or disappointed when their male partner says no. A lot of women might think, "Couldn't he get it together and try at least? I'm the one initiating, remember!"

However, feeling tired is the second most common reason men in my research report for turning down a sexual advance. For example, Alistair said, "When I'm really, really tired. The more physically exhausted I am, the less likely I am to feel sexual desire."

Another participant I spoke with said that he would not be in the mood for sexual activity after putting in a particularly long day at the office. Sometimes after one of those extra demanding days, all he was interested in was a nice cuddle with his wife: "There were times, and this is mostly when I worked fourteen- or sixteen-hour days sometimes, I would come home and she would be presenting herself to me, and I would just say, no I'm tired. And we would spend the night cuddling." Kaydan similarly described, "If you're really over tired, if you just drove all night to get home from a trip, or something, if you were flying. You come home, you don't feel like being intimate with someone because you're physically tired or, you know, not ready."

Ron expressed that he was sometimes conflicted when he started to feel some desire when he was tired. On the one hand, he described having a certain level of interest in sex, but ultimately, anticipating being even *more* exhausted the next day would end up outweighing his sexual interest. He stated,

> "It could also be just exhaustion, right? Like . . . if the kids make a squawk or something during the night, I get up and lay down with him or whatever. But I'm also getting up at 6 a.m. with them, 6:30 a.m. going to work. And it takes a toll. And there are times where, you know, I would like to be sexual with you right now, but my mind clicks in and it's like, you're exhausted now and if you guys stay up fooling around all night, do you know what tomorrow is going to be like?"

NO WINE, BUT FEELING FINE

However, as I mentioned previously, being sick or being *really* tired is the equivalent of saying no to that glass of wine because you're driving . . . or because it's 11 a.m. on a Tuesday. As women, we might not love the answer, but there are clear and understandable reasons for it. And these reasons make it *somewhat* easier for men to say no (and for women to accept that no). That's because they don't completely violate the idea of what it means to be a man who "should" always say yes to sex. These are the exceptions to the rule, if you will.

The more complex piece of the puzzle comes when men *want* to say no to sex but feel like they shouldn't—or even *couldn't*—say no. Those times when his answer, if only he could voice his thoughts honestly, would be "No, not tonight, honey." But he feels that he can't.

It's as though it's Saturday night, you don't have anything important to do the next morning, you haven't seen your friend in ages, and she offers you that glass of wine. But for some reason you still find yourself not really wanting it.

Then what?

Are Men "Allowed" to Not Want Sex?

In my research and in therapy I often ask men whether it's OK to say no to sex. Not just because they are sick or because they are tired. Are they "allowed" to just not want sex and to turn it down?

And, when worded like this, men often respond by saying, "Well, sure, of course it is" or "Yes, if anyone isn't in the mood for sex they should be able to say no." And I imagine that if I asked any woman the same question—is it OK for men to say no to sex?—she would say, "Yes, no one should have sex that they don't want to have."

But the question is intentionally hypothetical. It's hard to imagine anybody arguing that men shouldn't be allowed to say no to sexual advances. At least in theory. And maybe that's partially because we tend to think about those super-understandable reasons I just described: being sick or being really physically exhausted. But in practice holding on to this belief is much more challenging.

If the question is framed to women—are *you* OK with *your* male partner saying no when *you're* in the mood? When *you* want sex, when *you've* initiated, and he says no?—then it might not be *quite* so acceptable for him not to want it. Or at least women are more likely to feel a little wounded and to wonder what's going on. Because in real relationships there is the potential for feelings to get hurt, for dynamics and past interactions to show up, for power struggles to come into play, and for doubts and perceived expectations to influence.

So, after asking about whether men *in general* are allowed to say no, I get a little more personal. I ask my participant whether *he* can remember a time where he had said no to sex with a woman, his current female partner or someone in the past. Not whether it's OK for men in general to say no, but if *he* would ever do so or if he ever *has*. Because those are two potentially very different things.

Should we be allowed to have a party and not invite our friend's obnoxious new boyfriend? Sure, in theory. But when it comes down to it we will probably invite him to be socially polite and avoid insulting our friend.

As we know from the chapters The Motivation Myth and The Gender Myth, there are plenty of times (and plenty of reasons) that men may not be in the mood for sex. Which brings us to the next part of the *opportunity myth* equation: what happens when men don't really want sex? Do they go along with it anyway because that's what men do? Or do they perhaps say no?

SEX WITHOUT DESIRE

Have you ever consented to sex with your partner when you didn't *really* want it? To be clear, I'm not talking about being forced or coerced into anything that falls under the category of assault or abuse. I'm talking about being a fully consenting partner who just doesn't feel much desire but says yes to sex with your partner for any number of other reasons. For example, maybe it's been a while and you think you should just get it on before another few days pass. Or your partner has been all sorts of sweet recently and you just want to throw them a bone. Literally.

It could look something like this: You're lying in bed with your partner reading. They move in and start to kiss you and make moves toward having sex. You're pretty into your book and did not have sex on the brain. But you say, "Meh, why not," and start getting it on anyway.

I'm going to assume that any *woman* reading this has done this. In fact, there is an entire model of women's sexual response that revolves around this premise.[1] That is, the idea that many women (or even all women at some time) have sex *before* their desire kicks in. Women agree to sex, then, as they make out or touch their partner, desire may (or may not) start to creep in.[2] And they decide how or whether they want to continue.

But how often are *men* in this situation? Where *they* aren't feeling much (if any) desire, where they aren't that interested in having sex, but can tell their partner is so they say, "Meh, I guess"?

Well, probably a lot more often than we acknowledge.

Sexual compliance is a term that refers to the act of *willingly* engaging in sexual activity without feeling desire.[3] It's crucial to note that sexual compliance is *entirely* different from what has been termed *token resis-*

tance (i.e., saying no to sex when one really means yes)[4] and instances where an individual is forced into sexual intercourse without consent, as in the case of rape.[5] Rather, sexual compliance acknowledges that in an intimate relationship it is rare (dare I say impossible?) for both of us to *always* feel sexual desire at the same time. As a result, one of us may engage in sexual activity with our partner, completely willingly and in order to make the other happy, but without feeling sexual desire ourselves.

So, how often are women and men reporting that they engage in sexual compliance?

In what is, in my opinion, *the* groundbreaking study on debunking norms about men and sex, researchers Lucia O'Sullivan and Sarah Vannier explored this phenomenon at the University of New Brunswick in Canada. Their study included sixty-three young men and women (aged eighteen to twenty-five) who were interviewed about instances of sexual compliance in the context of committed heterosexual relationships.[6] The participants were also asked to keep a record of the times they had sex over a three-week period and each time they were asked various questions about their motivations for sex and their satisfaction levels.

The findings?

Regardless of gender, almost half (46 percent) of participants reported at least one experience of sexual compliance over the time period with 17.2 percent of all sexual activity rated as sexually compliant.

Let's slow that down a little bit. Over a three-week period, *half* of the men and *half* of the women reported consenting to sex without desire and almost one out of every five sexual encounters included (at equal rates) the man or woman consenting to sex they didn't desire.

As a woman I'm hardly surprised at the rates of sexual compliance among female participants. However, the finding that *men's* sexual compliance was *just* as frequent as women's reports goes against everything we've learned about men and sex. It runs counter to the idea that men would (or should) always be in the mood. That sex is always an appealing and exciting option for men. That men always have a reservoir of desire bubbling under the surface so they are ready to go at any time. And we certainly don't tend to think that men are having sex with their female partner as a favor to her.

What's more? Men (but *not* women) also reported *initiating* sexual activity even when they themselves were not feeling desire. I'll repeat that again: men reported initiating sexual activity even when they weren't in the mood for sex.

It's a fascinating concept, isn't it? That men might be initiating sex they don't even want. And that they are saying yes to sex they don't want.

So why might that be the case?

IT'S NOT WHAT MEN DO

While there are plenty of times where men say yes to sex when they definitely want it and are excited to have it, there are *also* times where social pressures, and pressures within intimate relationships, result in men saying yes to sex that they would prefer to say no to. In other words, being open to sexual encounters is sometimes a result of it being socially unacceptable to say no.

Throughout my research, participants described an awareness of cultural expectations that men should be constantly interested in sexual activity. As Dennis described, "The culturally expected norm is that [men] always want it and they're always ready for it."

And Luca shared that because men were *perceived* to want sex all the time, if they ever said no to sex, it could look suspicious. He said, "They tell us men that we think about sex all the time, so when we have somebody instigating it from the outside, now is the time to take advantage. It's allegedly what's more foremost in your mind."

One man I spoke with perceived that it would be problematic for him to say no to sexual activity because men normally initiate. He believed saying no could lead to his female partner questioning his masculinity: "Because we're always complaining that we're not getting enough sex, if they initiate it, and then all of a sudden we're saying no to them? Then it's like 'What's your problem? You're not a real man,' type of thing."

Despite knowing and critically thinking about the masculine norms, one man I talked to still found himself thinking about them when having sex with this wife:

> "Even in my own relationship, when I say no to sex, and I do, it's not always her; there is a part of me that feels guilt. Like, you know, if she wants to have sex and I don't and I say no, I feel guilty. Even though she doesn't expect me to and she tries to stop me from feeling that way, I feel it anyway . . . that comes from a big social construct that

says I should want to have sex with anyone who wants to have sex with me."

It seems, therefore, that men are so aware of what is expected of them—those social norms we've been talking about throughout this book—that they sometimes feel they need act in a way that aligns with those expectations, even when their true experiences run counter.

As a quick, but *very* important aside: recent research has documented that young, college-age men are engaging in unwanted and even *nonconsensual* sex because they fear they would be "unmanly" if they said no to a woman who wanted to have sex with them.[7]

HER FEELINGS WOULD BE HURT

The social and masculinity piece addresses the norms that exist "out there" and impact the way men "should" behave. Sometimes these norms are viewed critically and at a distance, and other times they are internalized.

However, I'm a relationship therapist, and the focus of this book is what happens with sex *within* an intimate relationship. And that's because separate from what is happening out there, we get to come up with our *own* rules and norms for what works and what doesn't in our own intimate relationships. And from my experience it's what men's female partners think (or what men *think* she thinks) that plays the biggest roles in men's sexual behaviors. In other words, above and beyond social messages men receive about demonstrating their desire, men are more concerned about how their female partner would react if he said no to her sexual advances.

If you recall from The Rejection Myth chapter, sexual rejection was found to be hurtful for both men and women.[8] Yet while I argued that we tend to minimize or downplay the hurt that *men* experience from rejection, we tend to accept and recognize how much sexual rejection can hurt for women. And most men know this. Either a man *has* rejected his partner's sexual advances in the past and could see how much it hurt her, or he can *imagine* how she would react if he said no. Either way, men tend to suggest that, if possible, they want to avoid causing their partners the hurt of saying no to sex when she initiates.

When asked about their reasons for having sex they did not desire, male participants in the O'Sullivan and Vannier study described previously indicated it was because they did not want to hurt their female partner's feelings.[9] And in my own interviews with men, it regularly and reliably comes up that their female partner was the main source of pressure men felt to say yes to sex. Specifically, out of desire to appear manly or "normal" to their female partners, some men talked about feigning an interest in sex, or having sex without desire, in order to keep up appearances. For example,

> "It's keeping up appearances for my wife at least. Because to some extent I think she buys into the stereotype that men are more sexually active or have more sexual desire. So if I'm not doing that, I think she feels sexually inadequate? So sometimes I'll feign sexual desire even if I'm not into it just so she feels good about herself."

And another said,

> "I think she would probably be upset. I think because she knows that my desire level is a lot higher than hers, typically, that she would be upset. She would think something is wrong. And she knows me, my personality, she knows this about me. So she would think something weird is going on if I said no I don't want to."

Because they wanted to make their female partners happy, or at least to avoid causing any strain in the relationship, a number of men I've spoken with have described saying yes to sexual activity to avoid eliciting any negative emotional consequences. Levi described his experience of saying yes to his wife's sexual advances as motivated by desire to protect her feelings, rather than from a place of sexual interest:

> "My wife has very low self-esteem. She is very self-conscious about her body. She's a little overweight; I don't care. So if I was to say no to her, it's happened before, so I know what happens. She thinks that she's not desirable, she's not attractive or whatever. So it's one of those things where I have to think of her feelings. If I'm going to say no, what's going to happen to her, like, what her feeling is going to be like afterward."

And Shay said that if he turned down his wife's sexual advances it would hurt her feelings and he felt that saying no to sex was not worth upsetting her. He said,

> "It's definitely tough to say no. Because I've always been a people pleaser in general. And so it's tough to say no in general for me. But also because it's your partner, your wife, and you want to make them happy. So yeah, anytime you say no you feel bad. I haven't had to do that very much."

APPROACHING: I, AVOIDING: 0

There is a plethora of reasons we may choose to have sex with our partner. If you remember that awesome study I described in The Gender Myth chapter, there are at least 237 documented reasons men and women have sex![10] And the reasons that we have sex matter, in terms of how satisfied we are sexually and relationally.

Relationship researchers at the University of Toronto explored men's and women's motivations for having, and not having, sex. And they divided these reasons into two categories: *avoidance goals* and *approach goals*.[11] Approach goals are reasons that you have sex that enhance intimacy in your relationship. They are inherently positive. You want to feel close. You want to say thank you because your partner made you a delicious dinner or picked up flowers for you on their way home. Or they look super cute and you're not necessarily turned on but are still more than happy to go along with sex if they are interested.

Then there are avoidance goals. Avoidance goals are reasons we have sex, but they come from a desire to, well, *avoid* a negative reaction from our partner. It would be like having sex because we worried our partner would be mad at us if we didn't. Or if they pouted. Or got sad. Or didn't have sex with us the next time we wanted it, or . . . you get the idea.

What this all boils down to is that having sex to *avoid* your partner being upset is likely leading to lower sexual satisfaction and ultimately lower relationship satisfaction. Simply put, we want to avoid avoidance goal sex.

WHY THIS MYTH IS A PROBLEM

The myth that men should say yes to any sexual opportunity that comes their way is detrimental to relationships. It reinforces the idea that men are void of any deep emotions (i.e., "Get over your sadness/stress/worry because sex should fix everything!"). And, additionally, when men *do* say no to sex and we believe that runs counter to what men *should* do, it can leave men feeling unnecessary and perplexed and women feeling unnecessarily hurt and doubting themselves—sexually, personally, and relationally.

Women: No one likes having their sexual advances rejected. It just doesn't feel great no matter how you cut it. However, if we believe the myth that men *should* take any sexual opportunity that comes their way, then when they do say no to our advances (even just that *one* time), we tend to take that *very* personally.

However, it is completely normal for a man's interest to ebb and flow and for him to not want to have sex even when you're interested. This isn't cause for panic, it's just normal human experience and variation. Further, most often when men turn down sex it probably has nothing to do with you. I'm going to repeat that again: when men say no to sex, it most likely has *nothing* to do with you. Your partner may feel sick. He might be tired. He might be distracted and stressed. So try not to take it personally. It's always worth being curious and asking questions if it's a pattern (i.e., as we discussed in The Motivation Myth chapter, there are several reasons men may not be in the mood for sex, including illness, severe stress, and such), but a no here and there does not require sending off the alarm bells.

Also, if your partner *does* turn down sex when you suggest it, consider responding the same way you would like him to respond when *you're* not in the mood. Pouting, getting angry, or being defensive are never good options; they make the other person feel bad and may even lead your partner to concede to having sex to avoid a negative reaction (a big no-no for sexual satisfaction according to the research I shared earlier). Instead, ask if everything is OK, tell him it's alright that he doesn't want to have sex, see if cuddling or snuggling is an option instead, and wait for the next time a better opportunity presents itself.

Men: First and foremost: it's completely, 110 percent OK to say no to sex, even if your wife or girlfriend wants it. It does not mean you are any less of a man, and it *certainly* doesn't mean that there is anything wrong with you. Saying no to sex in a longer-term relationship can feel like a jarring experience for a lot of men the first time it happens (and it's not necessarily any easier moving forward). But it's natural, it's normal, and there is no reason to panic!

While it's perfectly OK to have sex sometimes for your partner (on both ends, and when kept balanced and for healthy, relationship enhancing reasons), we don't want to get in the habit of frequently having sex that we're not that excited about, or flat-out don't want. It's better to just explain to your partner what's going on and that you're not in the mood. If she initiates sex and you're not in the mood, try letting her down the same way *you* would want to be turned down. Provide some validation, an explanation, and suggest another time to get intimate. For example, "You look beautiful. I love having sex with you but I'm just so wiped today. Can we try in the morning instead?" And take it upon yourself to initiate the next time.

MYTH IN ACTION: CHERYL AND JASON

The Case of the Red Lace Teddy

Back to Cheryl and Jason.

Cheryl and Jason were in their late forties. They met at a sports bar just over fifteen years earlier. Cheryl was serving drinks and Jason was watching the game, but said he found himself more interested in chatting with Cheryl when she came by with the next round than which team was scoring touchdowns.

The two hit it off right away. There was a connection. They talked easily and the sex was pretty good too. Then they got married and moved in together and things changed. Their sexual frequency decreased, and they just started to focus on other stuff. They had more responsibilities. Cheryl was unhappy at work. Jason's father had been diagnosed with Alzheimer's. Life just got a whole lot harder.

And in the midst of all this Cheryl bought that red lace teddy to spice things up and bring the focus back to the couple again. But, unfortunately, Jason wasn't there. He was still thinking about all the other stressful things going on. And, unlike other times, *this* time he did not find sex to be a reliever for that stress. He turned inward and Cheryl felt it. She missed him and was reaching out—with words, with actions, and then that red lace teddy that went unnoticed.

So now that everything was out there we were able to talk through the real reason Jason said no that night. We had to work through years of beliefs and built-up insecurities about it being about Cheryl, her appearance, his feelings toward her, and his lack of sexual interest. We had to revisit the memory so that Cheryl could understand that Jason was distracted and worried about plenty of other life events and that these were reasons he missed her sexual cues.

We also worked on Cheryl's need to be really *seen* again by Jason. To accept that he still sexually desired her. That he truly found her attractive. This took a long time. Fifteen years of believing your partner isn't very sexually turned on by you will do a lot of damage. We encouraged Jason to regularly and explicitly share his sexual attraction for Cheryl when he felt it; and for Cheryl to try and slowly let it sink in and feel it.

But most importantly, we had to address how Cheryl could put herself back out there and again initiate sex in the relationship after all these years. We started slow and steady. Cheryl had to know that when she took the risk to initiate sex, it was going to work out. She couldn't risk a no again, not yet at least. So we came up with a system where Jason indicated that he was in the mood (by wearing a certain go-to plaid shirt that Cheryl really liked). When he wore it, it was a sign that he was in the mood for sex, and if Cheryl also felt in the mood, she would know she could make a move and Jason would be ready for her.

And we agreed that over time as her confidence levels increased, they would both work on building some resiliency so that they could both say no without it being detrimental to the other person. We encouraged Cheryl to remember that when Jason said no, it was not a reflection of his lack of attraction and it did not mean anything was terribly wrong on his end. Jason agreed he would tell Cheryl why he wasn't in the mood when this happened (i.e., that he was tired, sick, distracted, not horny) to reassure Cheryl it was not personal, and then the ball would be in his court to initiate the next time.

SUMMARY

There is a widely held belief that because men always want sex, they should happily take any opportunity that comes their way. However, sometimes men may prefer to say no to sex, but struggle when they don't live up to certain norms and expectations.

- The belief that men never turn down a sexual opportunity is so pervasive that even men sometimes report never saying no to sex.
- However, there are plenty of reasons men may turn down sex, including physical illness, exhaustion, and medical complications (which tend to be perceived as more acceptable reasons to say no to sex).
- Men report engaging in sexual compliance (having consensual sex with no desire) *just as frequently* as women do. In addition, they also report initiating sexual activity when they don't feel desire.
- Men indicate there is a perceived pressure to say yes to undesired sex, which comes from social pressures of what it means to be a man.
- However, men describe that the biggest source of pressure to say yes to sexual opportunities is to avoid upsetting their female partner.
- Having sex to avoid a partner's negative reaction is found to result in decreased sexual and relationship satisfaction. Instead, it's highly recommended that men *and* women respect when their partner is not in the mood for sex and try again another time.

MYTH 10

The Masculinity Myth

THE "BRO" CODE

The chapters in this book essentially create what could be considered The Stereotypical Masculine Sexual Desire Code of Conduct. As a quick recap, that code of conduct includes the following:

1. Men's sexual desire is high and unwavering.
2. Men have higher sex drives than women.
3. Men's sexual desire is largely triggered by surface-level physical cues.
4. Men are primarily motivated by their own sexual gratification.
5. Pornography is integral to men's sex lives.
6. Men do the desiring; they don't need to feel desirable themselves.
7. Men pursue and initiate all sexual activity.
8. Sexual rejection doesn't hurt; men are used to it/must expect it.
9. Men will take any sexual opportunity that comes their way.

At this point, hopefully, you can look at this list and recognize that these nine propositions are, at minimum, far too simplified and, perhaps in some cases, completely false. You've also now seen how these limited rules for men and sex can work against our sexual satisfaction and intimate connections in a vast number of ways.

But if you recall, there is a "tenth commandment"—if you will—about men's sexual desire. That is

10. Real men are comfortable playing by these rules.

As you might have already noticed, this final chapter is a bit different from the others. You haven't been introduced to Jeremy and Amanda, or Tyson and Amelia, or any couple in therapy for that matter. That's because there is no nice and tidy case study for this myth. Because the topic addressed in this chapter has weaved its way throughout *every* topic we've talked about so far (and it shows up with nearly every couple I've worked with in therapy). That is, many men face an underlying pressure to demonstrate their sexual interest in order to *appear* to align with a narrow view of what our society currently deems to be "masculine" sexuality. As a result, there is an unfortunate discrepancy between men's true, authentic sexual experiences and what many men feel they need to (or "should") show to the world.

In this chapter we will explore how society in general, and male friends and acquaintances in particular, can play a profound role in reinforcing certain restrictive beliefs about men and sex. We will also explore how many men are critical of these limited norms and are ready for a change. And, most importantly, we will focus on how there is an opportunity for romantic, intimate relationships to be a place of respite and change from these restrictive social pressures. Specifically, I suggest that our romantic relationships offer an opportunity to completely rewrite our understanding of men and sex, and are the ultimate path to true, deep sexual intimacy.

THE RULES OF THE GAME

Biology and evolution play a role in sexual desire; there is no doubt. We know that from a biological standpoint, testosterone levels are somewhat (albeit complicatedly) related to levels of sexual desire.[1] We also can't underestimate the role of evolution when it comes to sex. As I described in The Origin of Myths chapter, our species—as all species on our planet—has evolved to procreate and pass on our genes.[2] It's how we've survived. And the human species has not only survived; it has *thrived*.

And our species has thrived because our ancestors chose the most successful mating strategies, which, theoretical evidence strongly suggests, included men having a more spontaneous sexual interested to reduce the chance of missing out on a mating opportunity.[3]

But that's not *all* that impacts desire—or almost any human behavior for that matter. Because we live in a society that requires us all to play by certain rules to get along and make the proverbial wheel turn. We are expected to be polite and patient at restaurants, hair salons, and banks, even when the staff is "in training" and being slow and making mistakes. We are asked to leave our underwear on when we try swimsuits and not to double-dip our chips at social gatherings. And we are expected to walk around with clothes on unless we're visiting a specially marked nudist beach or community. Some of these guidelines are enforced by law and some are enforced through social consequences—such as being well liked versus being eschewed from social interactions.

Social norms and standards dictate how we should behave and those expectations change by culture and by era.[4] Go to any baby shower today and you'll know within a millisecond what genitals the kid has. Pink for girls, blue for boys. But, fun fact: many years ago, pink was considered a dominant, bold, and masculine color that boys were dressed in (whereas girls were dressed in what was considered the more gentle, docile blue color).[5] Now, while it may not be uncommon for adult men to wear pink, you'd be hard-pressed to find parents dressing their newborn son in pastel pink onesies.

What I'm saying is that our social rules are very dominant, they can (and do) change, and whatever the rules are at any given time, we tend to play by them. So it's no stretch to suggest that social norms impact men's understanding of their sexual desire.

The questions are how? And to what degree?

MASS MARKETING (A LIMITED VERSION OF) MASCULINITY

Muscular men with huge bulges modeling "tighty-whities." Male singers with nearly naked women dancing and fawning over them. Buff and tough cowboys strutting to their giant (arguably phallic) trucks. Guys cracking a cold one, and then suddenly attracting the eyes of much more conventionally beautiful women. These images are not whizzing by men without their awareness. It's similar to how, despite women's best efforts, they have a hard time not noticing the waif-thin model with large, perky breasts modeling lingerie and internalizing that (unrealistic) standard of beauty. These messages, particularly when they are everywhere you turn, have a way of sticking with us.

And the images, advertisements, and messages catered to men tend to have one thing in common: the men are big, tough, dominant, and sexually charged, and are either (a) sexually turned on by attractive women at the drop of the hat or (b) already surrounded by said sexually attractive women. But what if these messages are having a negative impact on men? What if they are providing a limited idea of what men should be in general, and specifically with regard to their appetite for sex?

Interestingly enough, some of the men I've chatted with over the course of my research describe how the images frequently depicted in music videos convey a limited message to guys about what they "should" want. Richard, for example, said,

> "Look at the TV shows and the music videos, YouTube and stuff. Guys are supposed to be surrounded by women. Women aren't supposed to have their clothes on around them. Even that message speaks to . . . all guys want is naked women all around them all the time, right?"

It's not just visual images. Another of my participants, Charles, described that in addition to movies and shows, blogs, essays, and opinion articles also portray men's sexuality in limited ways. He said, "Whether in movies and TV or in editorials and essays, I've only ever seen male sexuality demonized and portrayed in a negative light. I have no idea how much damage this has done to multiple generations of men." And Noah similarly echoed that media is "doing men in general a disservice by oversimplifying their sexuality."

The way the media covers the topic of men and sex (or, perhaps more accurately, the *lack* of coverage on this topic outside of sexual assault and sexual abuse—important topics, no doubt, but in no way a nearly complete picture of men's sexuality) is also a source of misinformation. Men throughout my research seemed acutely aware that this one-dimensional note of men's desire was prevalent and impactful and lacked any complexity. As James said,

"I just feel that no one is talking about men's sexuality in any deep way. Whenever it is discussed in the media it's always negative and stereotypical ways. This narrative needs to change so men are allowed a fuller range of sexual expression."

James's comment hits me as particularly profound because it highlights two integral concerns. First, similar to most men I talk with, James echoes the sentiment that certain norms about men's desire are restrictive. But then he goes a bit further to suggest that until those norms change at a more *global* level, individual men aren't "allowed" to break from the norm. As if they did, there would be some serious negative social consequences.

So what would change on a more global level look like? Well, we can look to trends in advertising to start.

FROM WOMANIZING TO GENDER BENDING

Do you ever play the Unnecessarily Gendered Game? Maybe you know it. In my circle of friends we regularly make fun of products that are blatantly and, well, *unnecessarily* marketed to one gender. We try to spot the product and point it out first. Whether it's targeting girls with pink or princess-themed soap or candies or even grapes (yes, grapes!). Or, how at the time of writing this chapter, there was a lot of (negative) buzz around the lady Doritos that supposedly have a quieter crunch so women can be more comfortable and ladylike when eating in public![6] The Bic pens for ladies (because those other "manly" pens are just too big for women's dainty fingers!) is another example that received mass social criticism in part because of Ellen DeGeneres's infamous spoof on the product.[7]

There are also *numerous* products that are targeted toward men that are tone-deaf at best and insulting at worst. There seem to be companies that are worried the product wouldn't be palatable to men unless it was traditionally "manly" and masculine enough and completely separate from any feminine association. As a result some products are marketed toward men in a way that speaks to the lowest common denominator: men are sex crazed, so if you put "hot," sexually suggestive women beside *any* product, they'll jump. Think about the frequency with which nearly naked women are modeling beside cars, cologne, hamburgers, and beers, just to name a few examples.

If your mind goes to thinking critically about how we are using women's bodies to advertise, I fully agree. It's completely necessary to critically examine the use of female bodies to sell commercial goods. It's just that the other side of the coin is *also* worth exploring: do we think men are *that* surface level that they will buy a hamburger or beer because they see a sexy woman? What if we gave men a bit more credit than that?

It's worth noting that the culture of what we see on TV is changing, slowly. Or, perhaps more accurately, there are some exceptions to the rule that are beginning to stand out. The biggest brand marketing switch that caught my attention was Axe body spray. Not long ago their campaign was about average-looking guys attracting multiple incredibly gorgeous women once they sprayed themselves with this magical deodorant. One even implied a woman would leave her family and become a prostitute upon simply smelling the stuff.[8] Charming.

More recently, however, the campaign has switched to be more inclusive of men of various sizes and shapes, many going against the grain of the more stereotypical "macho," sex-crazed man previously depicted in commercials. And, further, through the commercials, the brand is encouraging men to embrace who they are—whether that means they have a big nose or like to dance in heels. The commercial seems to be reflecting a broader social change—it's not about the women you get or the size of your muscles; it's about being true to who you are. And the more we shift from men "only wanting one thing" to men just being their true authentic, complicated selves, the more positive impact we will likely see on men, masculinity, and how they interact with regard to sex.

The next time you're watching TV or flipping through a magazine in line at the store, pay attention to the messages that are being overtly, or even covertly, suggested about men and sex. And consider the impact these messages just might be having on men, women, and our intimate relationships.

DID YOU HEAR ABOUT JOHN AND SALLY?

Media, music videos, magazine articles, blogs, and commercials are one thing. But as the spheres of influence get closer to home, so too does the severity of impact. In the same vein, men also report being very aware and very impacted by what their guy friends are doing or, perhaps more accurately, what they *say* they are doing.

Admit it. We've all been there. We're out with some couple friends and they mention that they are going on another sunny vacation next month. And you think, "Didn't they *just* get back from somewhere hot?" And "When is the last time *we* went anywhere nice anyway?" Or you're talking about the division of labor in your household, and your friend casually drops that her partner always does the vacuuming, that she hasn't even touched it since they started dating. And you look at your partner and say, "When is the last time *you* vacuumed?" (completely ignoring that he cooks and your friend's partner doesn't—but that's neither here nor there). What I'm saying is that it's almost impossible not to compare our lives to our friends' lives. We use them as a point of comparison to evaluate how we are doing, where we want to do better, and where we aren't measuring up. More often than not these comparisons make us feel worse about ourselves. And, not surprisingly, the same thing happens in the goings on in the bedroom.

KEEPING UP WITH THE JONESES

In fact, I've talked with men who have outright described hearing other men talk about sexual experiences and that it makes them reconsider and reevaluate their own sex lives, often for the worse. One of my participants, Joel, worked in a male-dominated shop. He described his work-space like a stereotypical hockey locker room. It was full of men who talked freely and casually throughout the day, and sex came up a lot. He told me that he often found himself comparing his sexual experiences to the sexual stories his friends described at work, and often felt a little less than stellar after hearing other men brag about their sexcapades:

> "Guys can listen to what's going on at work, listen to their buddies claim what they did last night and everything else, and their thoughts are like . . . I should be doing that too . . . group mentality I guess. It seems to be the norm. And if you don't have that norm you try to get to that norm. And like I said . . . it's like he's getting some so I better be getting some, too."

In other words, even if Joel was feeling somewhat satisfied with where things were at with his sex life with his wife, he said that when his buddies started talking he felt differently about it. He would think: *Other men are getting sex. And want sex all the time. Maybe I should bump up my efforts a bit.*

If the influence of our culture of toxic masculinity was once elusive and difficult to grasp, it is certainly no longer the case. Most men I've spoken with can easily name the pressure they feel and act traditionally masculine with regard to sex. And it seems to be even more tangible when they can see it impacting their guy friends. As Collin said,

> "I think it's just the whole masculinity thing. It's guys not wanting to seem, almost, they think if they don't want it all the time they're somehow inferior or they're not going to look like a masculine male in front of their buddies or potentially in front of women as well. They want to show that they're like a young stallion or whatever."

More often than not when I ask men about their perceptions of *other* men's sexual desire, they share that men are behaving certain ways for show. They describe a facade that men put on to appear more stereotypically masculine. As one participant described, even making comments to girls could be forced because he said it's what men think they are supposed to do:

> "Men think that they're supposed to be making comments to a girl when they pass by, so they do. And I get the impression that a lot of it is forced. I think so at least . . . they're not as hopped up as they appear. But I think for men there is a role they need to fake desire that they don't necessarily have or make comments they wouldn't necessarily make. Especially maybe as they get older when they don't necessarily feel those comments anymore, they still want to be manly so they still drink a six-pack of beer and watch the Playboy channel because they think they're supposed to."

If you're aware of the cultural backlash to catcalls and women being told to smile when they walk down the street, you might, like me, be shuttering at a comment like this. To think that women could be harassed by (at least some) men who don't want to harass deep down but are doing it because they think they should? What an awful, sometimes toxic, cycle we're stuck in. But I digress . . .

The preceding quote is just one example, but these expectations have never been described to me in anything that resembles positive terms. They are always negative and even harmful. In fact, men who reported an awareness of traditional masculine norms and stereotypes often described these expectations as damaging and limiting to men. Listen to how Caleb put it:

> "There is a strong stereotype that men should want [sex] every time and maybe be able to perform three times in one night and stuff like that. And I think this is stupid and makes them really suffer. Act unnaturally. But they do not realize it, they would never confess, admit it. They say no this is what I want. It's stupid."

These men know there is a code of conduct when it comes to men and sex. Sometimes they are critical of it. And sometimes, despite their best efforts, they describe finding themselves impacted by those norms and expectations, particularly in the company of other men. But they are also, more often than not, critical of these norms, and even skeptical. And so desperate for them to change.

So how do we do that?

AN OPPORTUNITY

Taken together, these findings have significant implications for intimate heterosexual relationships. First, many men are suggesting that they are aware of social expectations about the way they *should* perform. And those pressures are coming at them from the media, social expectations, and interactions with other men. Second, some men say they are *more* likely to play into those roles when they are around their guy friends. They describe it almost like it's a game and they want to take a knee every now and then, but the ball keeps getting passed around and they take their turn playing by the rules. But what if *everyone* on the field wanted to call a time-out, and it's just that no one is willing to be the one to say it?

It's not to say guy friends aren't amazing and great. Actually, recent research is finding that men's close male friendships are actually closer and more intimate that they have ever been reported in the past.[9] And ultimately if we want to really challenge and change the way we think about men and sex, we have to work on these social and societal levels. But, as a starting point, if men want some respite, some reprieve from being "that guy," from being tough and always having to prove themselves, consider your romantic relationship as a potential safe haven to step away from all those expectations and pressures. To take off that armor. To bring down those walls. And for men to just be their truest, most authentic self with the woman they love.

WHAT DO WE WANT MOVING FORWARD?

As a society we are starved for a *real* conversation about men and sex that differs from the traditional stories we hear or things we have long assumed. I hope that at this point it's clear that men are far more complex than we have given them credit for, particularly when it comes to sex.

There is *nothing* wrong with some men having a high sex drive. My aim here isn't to flip things around and say that if men do want sex all the time or do feel their desire is high and constant there is something wrong with them. That goes against my whole argument. Men are half the population of the world, and I would never propose to say that one thing is true of over three billion people across the entire globe (and I wouldn't want anyone telling me about the way women are as if we all fall into one nice and tidy box!). Clearly there are variations and exceptions. However, for far too long the pendulum has been on the other side of the spectrum and far too many assumptions have been made without giving men the space to say whether they agree with those statements and whether they want to keep squeezing themselves into that restrictive, narrow mold.

Maybe some myths apply directly to your relationship while others don't. That's OK. Take what you can from this book. One myth might not resonate as deeply for you and your partner, while it might hit at the heart of the matter for another couple. My hope is that if even *one* of these myths makes you think differently about men and sex or the way you approach sex in your own intimate relationship, then I've done what I've set out to do. Because once myths about men and sex are confronted, people will often say things like "Yeah of course men don't *always* want sex, I meant *usually*, not *always*."

But each step in this direction helps us be clearer about what we *really* mean and what we *really* know when it comes to men and sex. My hope is to get the conversation going. To ask questions and move from a place of making assumptions based on outdated, yet omnipresent stereotypes and move to a state of genuine curiosity, full of new possibilities and a more authentic and holistic understanding of men and sex.

NOTES

INTRODUCTION

1. Rosemary Basson, "The Female Sexual Response: A Different Model," *Journal of Sex& Marital Therapy* 26, no. 1 (2000): 51–65.

2. William Simon and John Gagnon, "Sexual Scripts: Permanence and Change," *Archives of Sexual Behavior* 15, no. 2 (1986): 97–120.

3. Leonore Tiefer, "A New View of Women's Sexual Problems: Why New? Why Now?" *Journal of Sex Research* 38, no. 2 (2001): 89–96.

4. Sandra Byers, "Relationship Satisfaction and Sexual Satisfaction: A Longitudinal Study of Individuals in Long-Term Relationships," *Journal of Sex Research* 42, no. 2 (2005): 113–18.

THE ORIGIN OF MYTHS

1. Eric Corty and Jenay Guardiani, "Canadian and American Sex Therapists' Perceptions of Normal and Abnormal Ejaculatory Latencies: How Long Should Intercourse Last?" *Journal of Sex Medicine* 5, no. 5 (2008): 1251–56.

2. David Buss, "Psychological Sex Differences: Origins through Sexual Selection," *American Psychologist* 50, no. 3 (1995): 164–68.

3. David Buss, "Sexual Strategies Theory: Historical Origins and Current-Status," *Journal of Sex Research* 35, no. 1 (1998): 19–31.

4. Elaine Hatfield, Cherie Luckhurst, and Richard Rapson, "Sexual Motives: Cultural, Evolutionary, and Social Psychological Perspectives," *Sexuality & Culture* 14, no. 3 (2010): 173–90; Kevin MacDonald, "Warmth as a Developmental

Construct: An Evolutionary Analysis, *Child Development* 63, no. 4 (1992): 753–73.

5. William Simon and John Gagnon, "Sexual Scripts: Permanence and Change," *Archives of Sexual Behavior* 15, no. 2 (1986): 97–120; William Simon and John Gagnon, "Sexual Scripts: Origins, Influences and Change," *Qualitative Sociology* 26, no. 4 (2003): 491–97.

6. Michael Wiederman, "The Gendered Nature of Sexual Scripts," *Family Journal: Counseling and Therapy for Couples and Families* 13, no. 4 (2005): 496–502.

7. Deborah Toleman, *Dilemmas of Desire: Teenage Girls Talk about Sexuality* (Cambridge, MA: Harvard University Press, 2005).

8. Tatiana Masters, Erin Casey, Elizabeth Wells, and Diane Morrison, "Sexual Scripts among Young Heterosexually Active Men and Women: Continuity and Change," *Journal of Sex Research* 50, no. 5 (2013): 409–20; Wiederman, "The Gendered Nature of Sexual Scripts," 496–502.

9. Michael Kimmel, *The Gender of Desire: Essays on Male Sexuality* (Albany: State University of New York Press, 2005).

10. Kimmel, *The Gender of Desire*.

11. Will Courtenay, "Constructions of Masculinity and Their Influence on Men's Well-Being: A Theory of Gender and Health," *Social Science & Medicine* 50, no. 10 (2000): 1385–1401.

MYTH 1

1. Sarah Hunter Murray and Robin Milhausen, "Sexual Desire and Relationship Duration in Young Men and Women," *Journal of Sex & Marital Therapy* 38, no. 1 (2012): 28–40.

2. "Young Teens (12–14 Years of Age)," Centers for Disease Control and Prevention, last reviewed February 20, 2018.

3. Matt McMillen, "Low Testosterone: How Do You Know When Levels Are Too Low?" WebMD, accessed May 3, 2018.

4. Alvaro Morales, "Erectile Dysfunction: An Overview," *Clinics in Geriatric Medicine* 19, no. 3 (2003): 529–38.

5. Elaine Hatfield and Susan Sprecher, "Measuring Passionate Love in Intimate Relations," *Journal of Adolescence* 9, no. 4 (1986): 383–410.

6. Susan Sprecher and Pamela Regan, "Passionate and Companionate Love in Courting and Young Married Couples," *Sociological Inquiry* 68, no. 2 (1998): 163–85.

7. Elaine Hatfield and Richard Rapson, "Companionate Love Scale: Measurement Instrument Database for the Social Science," 2013. http://www.elaine

hatfield.com/pass_com.pdf DOI: http://dx.doi.org/10.13072/midss.484

8. Lori Brotto, "The DSM Diagnostic Criteria for Hypoactive Sexual Desire Disorder in Men," *Journal of Sexual Medicine* 7, no. 6 (2010): 2015–30.

9. American Psychiatric Association, *Diagnostic and Statistical Manual of Mental Disorders*, DSM-5. Arlington, VA: American Psychiatric Publishing, 2013.

10. Edward Laumann, Anthony Paik, and Raymond Rosen, "Sexual Dysfunction in the United States: Prevalence and Predictors," *JAMA* 281, no. 6 (1999): 537–44.

11. Bente Traeen, Monica Martinussen, Katarina Oberg, and Hakon Kavli, "Reduced Sexual Desire in a Random Sample of Norwegian Couples," *Sexual and Relationship Therapy* 22, no. 3 (2007): 303–22.

12. Raymond Rosen, "Prevalence and Risk Factors of Sexual Dysfunction in Men and Women," *Current Psychiatry Reports* 2, no. 3 (2000): 189–95.

13. Brotto, "The DSM Diagnostic Criteria," 2015–30.

14. Rosen, "Prevalence and Risk Factors," 189–95.

15. Annie Potts, Nicola Gavey, Victoria Grace, and Tiina Vares, "The Downside of Viagra: Women's Experiences and Concerns," *Sociology of Health & Illness* 25, no. 7 (2003): 697–719.

MYTH 2

1. Rosemary Basson, "Using a Different Model of Female Sexual Response to Address Women's Problematic Low Sexual Desire," *Journal of Sex & Marital Therapy* 27, no. 5 (2001): 395–403.

2. Cindy Meston and David Buss, "Why Humans Have Sex," *Archives of Sexual Behavior* 36, no. 4 (2007): 477–507.

3. Meston and Buss, "Why Humans Have Sex," 477–507.

4. Janet Hyde, "The Gender Similarity Hypothesis," *American Psychologist* 60, no. 6 (2005): 581–92; Janet Hyde, "New Directions in the Study of Gender Similarities and Differences," *Association for Psychological Science* 16, no. 5 (2007): 259–63.

5. Roy Baumeister, Kathleen Catanese, and Kathleen Vohs, "Is There a Gender Difference in Strength of Sex Drive? Theoretical Views, Conceptual Distinctions, and a Review of Relevant Evidence," *Personality and Social Psychology Review* 5, no. 3 (2001): 242–73.

6. Baumeister, Catanese, and Vohs, "Is There a Gender Difference in Strength of Sex Drive?" 242–73.

7. Michele Alexander and Terri Fisher, "Truth and Consequences: Using the Bogus Pipeline to Examine Sex Differences in Self-Reported Sexuality," *Journal of Sex Research* 40, no. 1 (2007): 27–35.

8. Stephanie Davies, Jennifer Katz, and Joan Jackson, "Sexual Desire Discrepancies: Effects on Sexual and Relationship Satisfaction in Heterosexual Dating Couples," *Archives of Sexual Behavior* 28, no. 6 (1999): 553–67.

9. Kristen Mark and Sarah Murray, "Gender Differences in Desire Discrepancy as a Predictor of Sexual and Relationship Satisfaction in a College Sample of Heterosexual Romantic Relationships," *Journal of Sex & Marital Therapy* 38, no. 2 (2012): 198–215.

10. BBC News, "Women 'More Likely to Lose Interest in Sex,'" September 14, 2017.

11. Amy Muise, Sarah Stanton, James Kim, and Emily Impett, "Not in the Mood? Men Under- (Not Over-) Perceive Their Partner's Sexual Desire in Established Relationships," *Journal of Personality and Social Psychology* 110, no. 5 (2016): 725–42.

12. Mark and Murray, "Gender Differences in Desire Discrepancy," 198–215.

MYTH 3

1. Elaine Hatfield, Cherie Luckhurst, and Richard Rapson, "Sexual Motives: Cultural, Evolutionary, and Social Psychological Perspectives," *Sexuality & Culture* 14, no. 3 (2010): 173–90.

2. Cindy Meston and David Buss, "Why Humans Have Sex," *Archives of Sexual Behavior* 36, no. 4 (July 2007): 477–507.

3. David Fredrick, Janet Lever, Brian Joseph Gillespie, and Justin Garcia, "What Keeps Passion Alive? Sexual Satisfaction Is Associated with Sexual Communication, Mood Setting, Sexual Variety, Oral Sex, Orgasm, and Sex Frequency in a National U.S. Study," *Journal of Sex Research* 54, no. 2 (2017): 186–201.

4. Rosemary Basson, "The Female Sexual Response: A Different Model," *Journal of Sex & Marital Therapy* 26, no. 1 (2000): 51–65.

5. Anthony Bogaert and Lori Brotto, "Object of Desire Self-Consciousness Theory," *Journal of Sex & Marital Therapy* 40, no. 4 (2014): 323–38.

6. Sarah Hunter Murray and Robin Milhausen, "Factors Impacting Women's Sexual Desire: Examining Long-Term Relationship in Emerging Adulthood," *Canadian Journal of Human Sexuality* 21, no. 2 (2012): 101–15.

MYTH 4

1. Tatiana Masters, Erin Casey, Elizabeth Wells, and Diane Morrison, "Sexual Scripts among Young Heterosexually Active Men and Women: Continuity and Change," *Journal of Sex Research* 50, no. 5 (2013): 409–20.

2. Will Courtenay, "Constructions of Masculinity and Their Influence on Men's Well-Being: A Theory of Gender and Health," *Social Science & Medicine* 50, no. 10 (2000): 1385–1401.

3. Sara Chadwick and Sari van Anders, "Do Women's Orgasms Function as Masculinity Achievement for Men?" *Journal of Sex Research* 54, no. 9 (2017): 1141–52.

4. Chadwick and van Anders, "Do Women's Orgasms Function as Masculinity Achievement for Men?" 1141–52.

5. Laurie Mintz, *Becoming Cliterate*: *Why Orgasm Equality Matters and How to Get It* (San Francisco: HarperOne, 2017).

6. Emily Nagoski, *Come as You Are: The Surprising New Science That Will Transform Your Sex Life* (New York: Simon & Schuster, 2015).

7. Lori Brotto, *Better Sex through Mindfulness: How Women Can Cultivate Desire* (Vancouver: Greystone Books, 2018).

8. Leonore Tiefer, "A New View of Women's Sexual Problems: Why New? Why Now?" *Journal of Sex Research* 38, no. 2 (2001): 89–96.

MYTH 5

1. Strange But True, "How Big Is the Porn Industry?" Medium, February 19, 2017.

2. "Pornhub's 2016 Year in Review," Pornhub, January 4, 2017.

3. Erik Janssen, Kimberly McBride, William Yarber, Brandon Hill, and Scott Butler, "Factors That Influence Sexual Arousal in Men: A Focus Group Study," *Archives of Sexual Behavior* 37, no. 2 (2008): 252–65.

4. Janssen et al., "Factors That Influence Sexual Arousal in Men," 252–65.

5. Megan Mass, Sara Vasilenko, and Brian Willoughby, "A Dyadic Approach to Pornography Use and Relationship Satisfaction among Heterosexual Couples: The Role of Pornography Acceptance and Anxious Attachment," *Journal of Sex Research* 55, no. 7 (2018): 1–11.

6. David Ley, *The Myth of Sex Addiction* (Lanham, MD: Rowman & Littlefield, 2012).

MYTH 6

1. Sarah Hunter Murray and Robin Milhausen, "Factors Impacting Women's Sexual Desire: Examining Long-Term Relationship in Emerging Adulthood," *Canadian Journal of Human Sexuality* 21, no. 2 (2012): 101–15.

2. Murray and Milhausen, "Factors Impacting Women's Sexual Desire," 101–15.

3. Rosemary Basson, "Using a Different Model of Female Sexual Response to Address Women's Problematic Low Sexual Desire," *Journal of Sex & Marital Therapy* 27, no. 5 (2001): 395–403.

4. Anthony Bogaert and Lori Brotto, "Object of Desire Self-Consciousness Theory," *Journal of Sex & Marital Therapy* 40, no. 4, (2014): 323–38.

5. Bogaert and Brotto "Object of Desire Self-Consciousness Theory," 323–38.

6. Erik Janssen, Kimberly McBride, William Yarber, Brandon Hill, and Scott Butler, "Factors That Influence Sexual Arousal in Men: A Focus Group Study," *Archives of Sexual Behavior* 37, no. 2 (2008): 252–65.

7. Helene Shugart, "Managing Masculinities: The Metrosexual Moment," *Communication and Critical/Cultural Studies* 5, no. 3 (2008): 280–300.

MYTH 7

1. William Simon and John Gagnon, "Sexual Scripts: Permanence and Change," *Archives of Sexual Behavior* 15, no. 2 (1986): 97–120.

2. Shari Dworkin and Lucia O'Sullivan, "Actual versus Desired Initiation Patterns among a Sample of College Men: Tapping Disjunctures within Traditional Male Sexual Scripts," *Journal of Sex Research* 42, no. 2 (2005): 150–58.

3. Tatiana Masters, Erin Casey, Elizabeth Wells, and Diane Morrison, "Sexual Scripts among Young Heterosexually Active Men and Women: Continuity and Change," *Journal of Sex Research* 50, no. 5 (2013): 409–20.

4. Michael Wiederman, "The Gendered Nature of Sexual Scripts," *Family Journal* 13, no. 4 (2005): 496–502.

5. Masters et al., "Sexual Scripts among Young Heterosexually Active Men and Women," 409–20.

6. William Simon and John Gagnon, "Sexual Scripts: Origins, Influences and Changes," *Qualitative Sociology* 26, no. 4 (2003): 491–97.

7. Sarah Hunter Murray, Robin Milhausen, Cynthia Graham, and Leon Kuczynski, "A Qualitative Exploration of Factors That Affect Sexual Desire among

Men Aged 30 to 65 in Long-Term Relationships," *Journal of Sex Research* 54, no. 3 (2016): 319–30.

8. Robin Milhausen and Edward Herold, "Does the Sexual Double Standard Still Exist? Perceptions of University Women," *Journal of Sex Research* 36, no.4 (1999): 361–68.

9. Dworkin and O'Sullivan, "Actual versus Desired Initiation Patterns," 150–58.

10. Dworkin and O'Sullivan, "Actual versus Desired Initiation Patterns," 150–58.

11. Amy Muise, Sarah Stanton, James Kim, and Emily Impett, "Not in the Mood? Men Under- (Not Over-) Perceive Their Partner's Sexual Desire in Established Relationships," *Journal of Personality and Social Psychology* 110, no. 5 (2016): 725–42.

MYTH 8

1. Hanneke de Graaf and Theo Sandfort, "Gender Differences in Affective Responses to Sexual Rejection," *Archives of Sexual Behavior* 33, no. 4 (August 2004): 395–403.

2. de Graaf and Sandfort, "Gender Differences," 401.

3. Sarah Hunter Murray, Robin Milhausen, Cynthia Graham, and Leon Kuczynski, "A Qualitative Exploration of Factors That Affect Sexual Desire among Men Aged 30 to 65 in Long-Term Relationships," *Journal of Sex Research* 54, no. 3 (May 2016): 319–30.

4. Brené Brown, "The Power of Vulnerability," TEDx video, June 2010.

5. Brené Brown, *The Gifts of Imperfection: Let Go of Who You Think You're Supposed to Be and Embrace Who You Are* (Centre City, MN: Hazelden Publishing, 2010); Brené Brown, *I Thought It Was Just Me (But It Isn't): Telling the Truth about Perfectionism, Inadequacy, and Power* (New York: Avery, 2007).

6. Brené Brown, *Daring Greatly: How the Courage to Be Vulnerable Transforms the Way We Live, Love, Parent, and Lead* (New York: Gotham Books, 2012), 34.

7. Brown, *Daring Greatly*, 102–3.

8. Amy Muise, Sarah Stanton, James Kim, and Emily Impett, "Not in the Mood? Men Under- (Not Over-) Perceive Their Partner's Sexual Desire in Established Relationships," *Journal of Personality and Social Psychology* 110, no. 5 (2016): 725–42.

9. Sarah Hunter Murray, "Women's Sexual Desire: Examining Long-Term Relationships in Emerging Adulthood" (master's thesis, University of Guelph, 2010).

MYTH 9

1. Rosemary Basson, "The Female Sexual Response: A Different Model," *Journal of Sex & Marital Therapy* 26, no. 1 (2000): 51–65.

2. Rosemary Basson, "Using a Different Model of Female Sexual Response to Address Women's Problematic Low Sexual Desire," *Journal of Sex & Marital Therapy* 27, no. 5 (2001): 395–403; Rosemary Basson, "Women's Sexual Desire—Disordered or Misunderstood?" *Journal of Sex & Marital Therapy* 28, no. 1 (2002): 17–28.

3. Sarah Vannier and Lucia O'Sullivan, "Sex without Desire: Characteristics of Occasions of Sexual Compliance in Young Adults' Committed Relationships," *Journal of Sex Research* 47, no. 5 (2010): 429–39.

4. Charlene Muehlenhard, "Examining Stereotypes about Token Resistance to Sex," *Psychology of Women Quarterly* 35, no. 4 (2011): 676–83.

5. Emily Impett and Letitia Anne Peplau, "Why Some Women Consent to Unwanted Sex with a Dating Partner: Insights from Attachment Theory," *Psychology of Women Quarterly* 26, no. 4 (2002): 360–70.

6. Vannier and O'Sullivan, "Sex without Desire," 429–39.

7. Jessie Ford, "What about Young Men Who Are Having Unwanted Sex?" *The Conversation*, January 3, 2018.

8. Hanneke de Graaf and Theo Sandfort, "Gender Differences in Affective Responses to Sexual Rejection," *Archives of Sexual Behavior* 33, no. 4 (August 2004): 395–403.

9. Vannier and O'Sullivan, "Sex without Desire," 429–39.

10. Cindy Meston and David Buss, "Why Humans Have Sex," *Archives of Sexual Behavior* 36, no. 4 (2007): 477–507.

11. Amy Muise, Emily Impett, and Serge Desmarais, "Getting It On versus Getting It Over With: Sexual Motivation, Desire, and Satisfaction in Intimate Bonds," *Personality and Social Psychology Bulletin* 39, no. 10 (October 2013): 1320–32.

MYTH 10

1. Sari van Anders, "Testosterone and Sexual Desire in Healthy Women and Men," *Archives of Sexual Behavior* 41, no. 5 (2012): 1471–84.

2. David Buss, "Psychological Sex Differences: Origins through Sexual Selection," *American Psychologist* 50, no. 3 (1995): 164–68.

3. David Buss, "Sexual Strategies Theory: Historical Origins and Current Status," *Journal of Sex Research* 35, no. 1 (1998): 19–31.

4. William Simon and John Gagnon, "Sexual Scripts: Permanence and Change," *Archives of Sexual Behavior* 15, no. 2 (1986): 97–120.

5. "When Did Girls Start Wearing Pink?" Smithsonian.com, accessed February 20, 2018.

6. Raisa Bruner, "The Internet Thinks 'Lady-Friendly' Doritos Are in Pretty Bad Taste," *Time*, updated February 6, 2018.

7. The Ellen Show, "Bic Pens for Women," YouTube video, October 12, 2012.

8. Keep Smiling, "Men Will Be Men New Ad 2017/Axe Prostitution Commercial 2017," YouTube video, January 30, 2017.

9. Stefan Robinson, Adam White, and Eric Anderson, "Privileging the Bromance: A Critical Appraisal of Romantic and Bromantic Relationships," *Men and Masculinities*, October 2017.

BIBLIOGRAPHY

Alexander, Michele, and Terri Fisher. "Truth and Consequences: Using the Bogus Pipeline to Examine Sex Differences in Self-Reported Sexuality." *Journal of Sex Research* 40, no. 1 (2007): 27–35, http://doi.10.1080/00224490309552164.

American Psychiatric Association. *Diagnostic and Statistical Manual of Mental Disorders*, DSM-5. Arlington, VA: American Psychiatric Publishing, 2013.

Basson, Rosemary. "The Female Sexual Response: A Different Model." *Journal of Sex & Marital Therapy* 26, no. 1 (2000): 51–65, http://doi:10.1080/009262300278641.

———. "Using a Different Model of Female Sexual Response to Address Women's Problematic Low Sexual Desire." *Journal of Sex & Marital Therapy* 27, no. 5 (2001): 395–403, http://doi:10.1080/713846827.

———. "Women's Sexual Desire—Disordered or Misunderstood?" *Journal of Sex & Marital Therapy* 28, no. 1 (2002): 17–28, http://doi:10.1080/009262302317250981.

Baumeister, Roy, Kathleen Catanese, and Kathleen Vohs. "Is There a Gender Difference in Strength of Sex Drive? Theoretical Views, Conceptual Distinctions, and a Review of Relevant Evidence." *Personality and Social Psychology Review* 5, no. 3 (2001): 242–73. http://doi:10.1207/S15327957PSPR0503_5.

BBC News. "Women 'More Likely to Lose Interest in Sex.'" September 14, 2017, http://www.bbc.com/news/health-41230891.

Bogaert, Anthony, and Lori Brotto. "Object of Desire Self-Consciousness Theory." *Journal of Sex & Marital Therapy* 40, no. 4 (2014): 323–38, http://doi:10.1080/0092623X.2012.756841.

Brotto, Lori. *Better Sex through Mindfulness: How Women Can Cultivate Desire*. Vancouver: Greystone Books, 2018.

———. "The DSM Diagnostic Criteria for Hypoactive Sexual Desire Disorder in Men." *Journal of Sexual Medicine* 7, no. 6 (2010): 2015–30, http://doi:10.1111/j.1743-6109.2010.01860.x.

Brown, Brené. *Daring Greatly: How the Courage to Be Vulnerable Transforms the Way We Live, Love, Parent, and Lead*. New York: Gotham Books, 2012.

———. *The Gifts of Imperfection: Let Go of Who You Think You're Supposed to Be and Embrace Who You Are*. Centre City, MN: Hazelden Publishing, 2010.

———. *I Thought It Was Just Me (but It Isn't): Telling the Truth about Perfectionism, Inadequacy, and Power*. New York: Avery, 2007.

———. "The Power of Vulnerability." TEDx video. June 2010, https://www.ted.com/talks/brene_brown_on_vulnerability.

Bruner, Raisa. "The Internet Thinks 'Lady-Friendly' Doritos Are in Pretty Bad Taste." *Time*, updated February 6, 2018, http://time.com/5133674/lady-doritos/.

Buss, David. "Psychological Sex Differences: Origins through Sexual Selection." *American Psychologist* 50, no. 3 (1995): 164–68, http://doi:19.1037/0003-066X.50.3.164.

———. "Sexual Strategies Theory: Historical Origins and Current Status." *Journal of Sex Research* 35, no.1 (1998): 19–31, http://doi:10.1080/00224499809551914.

Byers, Sandra. "Relationship Satisfaction and Sexual Satisfaction: A Longitudinal Study of Individuals in Long-Term Relationships." *Journal of Sex Research* 42, no. 2 (2005): 113–18. http://doi:10.1080/00224490509552264.

Centers for Disease Control and Prevention. "Young Teens (12–14 Years of Age)." Last reviewed February 20, 2018, https://www.cdc.gov/ncbddd/childdevelopment/positive parenting/adolescence.html.

Chadwick, Sara, and Sari van Anders. "Do Women's Orgasms Function as Masculinity Achievement for Men?" *Journal of Sex Research* 54, no. 9 (2017): 1141–52, http://doi:10.1080/00224499.2017.1283484.

Corty, Eric, and Jenay Guardiani. "Canadian and American Sex Therapists' Perceptions of Normal and Abnormal Ejaculatory Latencies: How Long Should Intercourse Last?" *Journal of Sex Medicine* 5, no. 5 (2008): 1251–56, http://doi:10.1111/j.1743-6109.2008.00797.x.

Courtenay, Will. "Constructions of Masculinity and Their Influence on Men's Well-Being: A Theory of Gender and Health." *Social Science & Medicine* 50, no. 10 (2000): 1385–1401, http://doi:10.1016/S0277-9536(99)00390-1.

Davies, Stephanie, Jennifer Katz, and Joan Jackson. "Sexual Desire Discrepancies: Effects on Sexual and Relationship Satisfaction in Heterosexual Dating Couples." *Archives of Sexual Behavior* 28, no. 6 (1999): 553–67, http://doi:10.1023/A:1018721417683.

de Graaf, Hanneke, and Theo Sandfort. "Gender Differences in Affective Responses to Sexual Rejection." *Archives of Sexual Behavior* 33, no. 4 (August 2004): 395–403, https://doi.org/10.1023/B:ASEB.0000028892.63150.be.

Dworkin, Shari, and Lucia O'Sullivan. "Actual versus Desired Initiation Patterns among a Sample of College Men: Tapping Disjunctures within Traditional Male Sexual Scripts." *Journal of Sex Research* 42, no. 2 (2005): 150–58, http://doi:10.2307/3813151.

The Ellen Show. "Bic Pens for Women." YouTube video, October 12, 2012, https://www.youtube.com/watch?v=eCyw3prIWhc.

Ford, Jessie. "What about Young Men Who Are Having Unwanted Sex?" *The Conversation*, January 3, 2018, https://theconversation.com/what-about-young-men-who-are-having-unwanted-sex-88677.

Fredrick, David, Janet Lever, Brian Joseph Gillespie, and Justin Garcia. "What Keeps Passion Alive? Sexual Satisfaction Is Associated with Sexual Communication, Mood Setting, Sexual Variety, Oral Sex, Orgasm, and Sex Frequency in a National U.S. Study." *Journal of Sex Research* 54, no. 2 (2017): 186–201, https://doi.org/10.1080/00224499.2015.1137854.

Hatfield, Elaine, Cherie Luckhurst, and Richard Rapson. "Sexual Motives: Cultural, Evolutionary, and Social Psychological Perspectives." *Sexuality & Culture* 14, no. 3 (2010): 173–90, http://doi: 10.1007/s12119-010-9072-z.

Hatfield, Elaine, and Richard Rapson. "Companionate Love Scale: Measurement Instrument Database for the Social Science" (2013). Retrieved from http://www.midss.org/content/companionate-love-scale (website); http://www.elainehatfield.com/pass_com.pdf (pdf of scale); http://dx.doi.org/10.13072/midss.484 (DOI).

Hatfield, Elaine, and Susan Sprecher. "Measuring Passionate Love in Intimate Relations." *Journal of Adolescence* 9, no. 4 (1986): 383–410, https://www.ncbi.nlm.nih.gov/pubmed/3805440.

Hyde, Janet. "The Gender Similarity Hypothesis." *American Psychologist* 60, no. 6 (2005): 581–92. http://doi:10.1037/0003-066X.60.6.581.

———. "New Directions in the Study of Gender Similarities and Differences." *Association for Psychological Science* 16, no. 5 (2007): 259–63. http://doi:10.1111/j.1467-8721.2007.00516.x.

Impett, Emily, and Letitia Anne Peplau. "Why Some Women Consent to Unwanted Sex with a Dating Partner: Insights from Attachment Theory." *Psychology of Women Quarterly* 26, no. 4 (2002): 360–70, http://doi:10.1111/1471-6402.t01-1-00075.

Janssen, Erik, Kimberly McBride, William Yarber, Brandon Hill, and Scott Butler. "Factors That Influence Sexual Arousal in Men: A Focus Group Study." *Archives of Sexual Behavior* 37, no. 2 (2008): 252–65, http://doi:10.1007/s10508-007-9245-5.

Keep Smiling. "Men Will Be Men New Ad 2017/Axe Prostitution Commercial 2017." You-Tube video, January 30, 2017, https://www.youtube.com/watch?v=c22zT_H6sF4.

Kimmel, Michael. *The Gender of Desire: Essays on Male Sexuality.* Albany: State University of New York Press, 2005.

Laumann, Edward, Anthony Paik, and Raymond Rosen. "Sexual Dysfunction in the United States: Prevalence and Predictors." *JAMA* 281, no. 6 (1999): 537–44, https://www.ncbi.nlm.nih.gov/pubmed/10022110.

Ley, David. *The Myth of Sex Addiction.* Lanham, MD: Rowman & Littlefield, 2012.

MacDonald, Kevin. "Warmth as a Developmental Construct: An Evolutionary Analysis." *Child Development* 63, no. 4 (1992): 753–73, http://doi: 10.2307/1131231.

Mark, Kristen, and Julie Lassio. "Maintaining Sexual Desire in Long-Term Relationships: A Systematic Review and Conceptual Model." *Annual Review of Sex Research Special Issue* 55, nos. 4–5 (2018): 563–81, https://doi.org/10.1080/00224499.2018.1437592.

Mark, Kristen, and Sarah Murray. "Gender Differences in Desire Discrepancy as a Predictor of Sexual and Relationship Satisfaction in a College Sample of Heterosexual Romantic Relationships." *Journal of Sex & Marital Therapy* 38, no. 2 (2012): 198–215, http://doi: 10.1080/0092623X.2011.606877.

Mass, Megan, Sara Vasilenko, and Brian Willoughby. "A Dyadic Approach to Pornography Use and Relationship Satisfaction among Heterosexual Couples: The Role of Pornography Acceptance and Anxious Attachment." *Journal of Sex Research* 55, no. 6 (2018): 1–11, https://www.tandfonline.com/doi/abs/10.1080/00224499.2018.1440281.

Masters, Tatiana, Erin Casey, Elizabeth Wells, and Diane Morrison. "Sexual Scripts among Young Heterosexually Active Men and Women: Continuity and Change." *Journal of Sex Research* 50, no. 5 (2013): 409–420, http://doi:10.1080/00224499.2012.661102.

McMillen, Matt. "Low Testosterone: How Do You Know When Levels Are Too Low?" WebMD, accessed May 3, 2018, https://www.webmd.com/men/features/low-testosterone-explained-how-do-you-know-when-levels-are-too-low#1.

Meston, Cindy, and David Buss. "Why Humans Have Sex." *Archives of Sexual Behavior* 36, no. 4 (2007): 477–507, doi:10.1007/s10508-007-9175-2.

Milhausen, Robin, and Edward Herold. "Does the Sexual Double Standard Still Exist? Perceptions of University Women." *Journal of Sex Research* 36, no. 4 (1999): 361–68, http://doi:10.1080/00224499909552008.

Mintz, Laurie. *Becoming Cliterate: Why Orgasm Equality Matters and How to Get It.* San Francisco: HarperOne, 2017.

Morales, Alvaro. "Erectile Dysfunction: An Overview." *Clinics in Geriatric Medicine* 19, no. 3 (2003): 529–38, http://doi.org/10.1016/S0749-0690(02)00104-0.

Muehlenhard, Charlene. "Examining Stereotypes about Token Resistance to Sex." *Psychology of Women Quarterly* 35, no. 4 (2011): 676–83, htttp://doi.org/10.1177/0361684311426689.

Muise, Amy, Emily Impett, and Serge Desmarais. "Getting It On versus Getting It Over With: Sexual Motivation, Desire and Satisfaction in Intimate Bonds." *Personality and Social Psychology Bulletin* 39, no. 10 (October 2013): 1320–32, https://doi.org/10.1177/0146167213490963.

Muise, Amy, Sarah Stanton, James Kim, and Emily Impett. "Not in the Mood? Men Under- (Not Over-) Perceive Their Partner's Sexual Desire in Established Relationships." *Journal of Personality and Social Psychology* 110, no. 5 (2016): 725–42, http://doi:10.1037/pspi0000046.

Murray, Sarah Hunter. "Women's Sexual Desire: Examining Long-Term Relationships in Emerging Adulthood." Master's thesis, University of Guelph, 2010.

Murray, Sarah Hunter, and Robin Milhausen. "Factors Impacting Women's Sexual Desire: Examining Long-Term Relationship in Emerging Adulthood." *Canadian Journal of Human Sexuality* 21, no. 2 (2012): 101–15.

———. "Sexual Desire and Relationship Duration in Young Men and Women." *Journal of Sex & Marital Therapy* 38, no. 1 (2012): 28–40, http://doi:10.1080/0092623X.2011.569637.

Murray, Sarah Hunter, Robin Milhausen, Cynthia Graham, and Leon Kuczynski. "A Qualitative Exploration of Factors That Affect Sexual Desire among Men Aged 30 to 65 in Long-Term Relationships." *Journal of Sex Research* 54, no. 3 (May 2016): 319–30, http://dx.doi.org/10.1080/00224499.2016.1168352.

Nagoski, Emily. *Come as You Are: The Surprising New Science That Will Transform Your Sex Life*. New York: Simon & Schuster, 2015.

Pornhub. "Pornhub's 2016 Year in Review." January 4, 2017, https://www.pornhub.com/insights/2016-year-in-review.

Potts, Annie, Nicola Gavey, Victoria Grace, and Tiina Vares. "The Downside of Viagra: Women's Experiences and Concerns." *Sociology of Health & Illness* 25, no. 7 (2003): 697–719, https://doi.org/10.1046/j.1467-9566.2003.00366.x.

Robinson, Stefan, Adam White, and Eric Anderson. "Privileging the Bromance: A Critical Appraisal of Romantic and Bromantic Relationships." *Men and Masculinities*, October 2017, https://doi.org/10.1177/1097184X17730386.

Rosen, Raymond. "Prevalence and Risk Factors of Sexual Dysfunction in Men and Women." *Current Psychiatry Reports* 2, no. 3 (2000): 189–195, http://doi:10.1007/s11920-996-0006-2.

Shugart, Helene. "Managing Masculinities: The Metrosexual Moment." *Communication and Critical/Cultural Studies* 5, no. 3 (2008): 280–300, http://doi.org/10.1080/14791420802206833.

Simon, William, and John Gagnon. "Sexual Scripts: Origins, Influences and Changes." *Qualitative Sociology* 26, no. 4 (2003): 491–97, doi:10.1023/B:QUAS.0000005053.99846.e5.

———. "Sexual Scripts: Permanence and Change." *Archives of Sexual Behavior* 15, no. 2 (1986): 97–120, .

Smithsonian.com. "When Did Girls Start Wearing Pink?" accessed February 20, 2018, https://www.smithsonianmag.com/arts-culture/when-did-girls-start-wearing-pink-1370097/.

Sprecher, Susan, and Pamela Regan. "Passionate and Companionate Love in Courting and Young Married Couples." *Sociological Inquiry* 68, no. 2 (1998): 163–85, https://doi.org/10.1111/j.1475-682X.1998.tb00459.x.

Strange But True. "How Big Is the Porn Industry?" *Medium*, February 19, 2017, https://medium.com/@Strange_bt_True/how-big-is-the-porn-industry-fbc1ac78091b.

Tiefer, Leonore. "A New View of Women's Sexual Problems: Why New? Why Now? *Journal of Sex Research* 38, no. 2 (2001): 89–96, http://doi:10.1080/00224490109552075.

Toleman, Deborah. *Dilemmas of Desire: Teenage Girls Talk about Sexuality*. Cambridge, MA: Harvard University Press, 2005.

Traeen, Bente, Monica Martinussen, Katarina Oberg, and Hakon Kavli. "Reduced Sexual Desire in a Random Sample of Norwegian Couples." *Sexual and Relationship Therapy* 22, no. 3 (2007): 303–22, http://doi:10.1080/14681990701381203.

van Anders, Sari. "Testosterone and Sexual Desire in Healthy Women and Men." *Archives of Sexual Behavior* 41, no. 5 (2012): 1471–84, https://doi.org/10.1007/s10508-012-9946-2.

Vannier, Sarah, and Lucia O'Sullivan. "Sex without Desire: Characteristics of Occasions of Sexual Compliance in Young Adults' Committed Relationships." *Journal of Sex Research* 47, no. 5 (2010): 429–39, http://doi:10.1080/00224490903132051.

Wiederman, Michael. "The Gendered Nature of Sexual Scripts." *Family Journal: Counseling and Therapy for Couples and Families* 13, no. 4 (2005): 496–502, http://doi.org/10.1177/1066480705278729.

INDEX